THE CASSELL
BOOK OF PROVERBS

THE CASSELL BOOK OF
PROVERBS

Patricia Houghton

CASSELL

Cassell
Villiers House, 41/47 Strand
London WC2N 5JE

© Blandford 1981

First published 1981 as *A World of Proverbs* by
Blandford Press Limited
Cassell edition first published 1992

British Cataloguing-in-Publication Data
A catalogue entry for this book is available
from the British Library.

ISBN 0-304-34165-7

Printed and bound in Great Britain by Biddles Ltd, Guildford and King's Lynn

INTRODUCTION

THE PROVERBS TO be found in this book have been gleaned from many lands — some are familiar, others shrewd or perhaps rather cynical, even harsh. I hope there is something for everyone.

Every country, it seems, has its own version of the well-known, well-tried proverb. Here and there I have marked interesting comparisons. There is, for example, an echo of the 16th-century English proverb . . . 'You cannot make a silk purse out of a sow's ear' in the more prosaic version from Borneo: 'You may plant bitter cucumber on a bed of sago and manure it with honey, water it with treacle and train it to grow over sugar-cane; yet, when cooked, it will still be bitter to the taste'. Naturally we tend to use the shorter variety more in our everyday speech and conversation, but now and again a wise or subtle proverb sneaks in. It is at first surprising to note how many wise sayings and proverbs are quoted in the plays or films that most of us watch on television. If one reflects that many of these proverbs were being quoted three thousand years before Christ, one can see that they have been common currency for quite some time!

Proverbs put the salt, or the spice if you will, into conversation and speech; a little well-tried wisdom sometimes can make impact, and perhaps even lighten a difficult situation. How often do we all say 'More haste, less speed', or speed someone on their way warningly with, 'Take time to be quick'?

Perhaps proverbs are not really intended to be witty or clever and were first meant as warnings, but having been used throughout the passing of many generations they have gathered more than just wisdom. There is great satisfaction and even humour in many of them.

I have included a little folklore, old rhymes, and quotes by many famous people to give further interest — a book of alphabetical proverbs would be tedious. I hope that it may serve as a guide to some of the more uncommon proverbs as well as the familiar . . .

1
EVERYDAY PROVERBS

IN OUR EVERYDAY speech the use of proverbs is hardly noticed as they blend into the conversation so naturally — after all there is nothing quite like a proverb to emphasise or clarify a situation. Many small happenings occur during the course of a day, so many that we can be forgiven for not remembering them all. But what is almost certain is that most of us will have used a well tried proverb or two, and usually without realising.

—————————————— LATENESS ——————————————

To be late is a common everyday occurrence; the car will not start, the train is late, the bus does not run, or perhaps we over-sleep. In consequence we are late, and that inevitably brings a trite proverb or saying to someone's lips!

'A little too late, is much too late'
German

'Better late than never'

'It is not enough to run, one must start in time'
French

'Lose an hour in the morning, chase it all day'
Yiddish

and . . .

'He that riseth late must trot all day'
Benjamin Franklin

'Men count up the faults of those who keep them waiting'
French

'In vain they rise early that used to rise late'

or . . .

'Get a name to rise early, and you may lie all day'

And from Ambrose Bierce . . .
    'Better late than before anybody has invited you'

——————— ANGER ———————

As like as not, anger, or the anger of others, comes into our daily lives; wanting to provoke someone is a human failing, and there are some who cannot resist it . . .

'Many people lose their tempers merely from seeing you keep yours'

'An angry man is not fit to pray'
        Yiddish

'He who has been angry becomes cool again'
        Greek

'No man is angry that feels not himself hurt'
        Francis Bacon

'A tart temper never mellows with age; and a sharp tongue is the only edged tool that grows keener with constant use'

'All music jars when the soul's out of tune'

'Anger without power is folly'
        German
or . . .
'Anger can be an expensive luxury'
        Italian

'The tigers of wrath are wiser than the horses of instruction'
        William Blake

'There is no old age for a man's anger, only death'

'Anger as soon as fed is dead,
Tis starving makes it fat'
        Emily Dickinson

'Let not the sun go down upon your wrath'
        Bible

'When angry count four, when very angry, swear!'
        Mark Twain

TRUTH

The decision whether or not to tell the truth often weighs heavily upon us daily, sometimes perhaps it is kinder not to tell the whole truth. As a wise man unknown once said . . . 'A man that is wholly truthful can be cruel'

'Truth is stranger than fiction'

'All truth is not to be told at all times'

'Every truth has two sides; it is as well to look at both, before we commit ourselves to either'
  Aesop's Fables

'Truth has a handsome countenance but torn garments'
  German

'A lie travels round the world while truth is putting her boots on'
  French

'The truth is not always what we want to hear'
'How many will listen to the truth when you tell them?'
  Yiddish

'Time trieth truth'
  English

'In order that all men may be taught to speak the truth, it is necessary that all likewise should learn to hear it'
  Samuel Johnson

'Truth will out'
  Latin

'Truth and oil always come to the surface'
  Spanish

'The truth shall make you free'
  Bible

'Truth always lags last, limping along on the arm of time'

'Truth always arrives by the lame messenger'

'Pure truth, like pure gold, has been found unfit for circulation, because men have discovered that it is far more convenient to adulterate the truth than to refine themselves'
Charles Caleb Colton

ADVICE

And everyday we either give advice or take advice from someone else . . .

'Advice is a stranger, if welcome he stays for the night; if not welcome he returns the same day'
Malagasy

'There is nothing which we receive with so much reluctance as advice'
'Advice when most needed is least heeded'
English

'Write down the advice of him who loves you, though you like it not at present'
'Give neither counsel nor salt till you are asked for it'
Italian

'Good advice is often annoying, bad advice never'
French

'That is most true which we least care to hear'

'Advice should be viewed from behind'
Swedish

'An enemy will agree, but a friend will argue'
Russian

'God send me a friend that may tell me my faults; if not an enemy, and he surely will'

'Seek counsel of him who makes you weep, and not of him who makes you laugh'
Arabic

'When a man asks your advice, he usually tells you just how he expects you to decide'
Edgar Watson Howe

WISDOM

'The wisdom of others is sometimes irksome for they are constantly making us aware of it. But rest assured that such wisdom is often folly, for why else should they seek to belabour us?'
Anon

'A wise man may look ridiculous in the company of fools'

'The wise man sits on the hole in his carpet'
Persian

'A wise man hears one word and understands two'
Yiddish

'The heart of a wise man lies quiet like limpid water'
Cameroonian

'The wise man, even when he holds his tongue, says more than the fool when he speaks'
Yiddish

'The price of wisdom is above rubies'
Bible

'No wisdom like silence'

'Think with the wise but talk with the vulgar'
German

'Who knows most speaks least'
Spanish

'Do not talk Arabic in the house of a Moor'
Oriental

'Don't judge a man by the words of his mother, listen to the

comments of his neighbours'
Yiddish

'Wise men are like timber trees in a hedge, here and there one'

'He is not wise that is not wise for himself'
English

———— KNOWLEDGE & LEARNING ————

'Knowledge is power'

'He that increases knowledge increaseth sorrow'
Bible

'Knowledge comes, but wisdom lingers, and he bears a
laden breast,
Full of sad experience moving towards the stillness
of his rest . . .'
Alfred, Lord Tennyson

'A table is not blessed if it has fed no scholars'
Yiddish

'The world would perish if all men were learned'

'Learn as though you would never be able to master it;
Hold it as though you would be in fear of losing it'
Confucius

An old Sanskrit proverb . . .
'The learning of books that you do not make your own
wisdom is money in the hands of another in time of need'

'Learning without thought is labour lost;
Thought without learning is perilous'
Confucius

'He who does not know one thing knows another'
Kenyan

'A little knowledge is a dangerous thing'

'As we live, so we learn'
Yiddish

'We live and learn'
English

'Learning is there for every man'
French

'Learning . . . the kind of ignorance distinguishing the studious'
Ambrose Bierce

AMBITIONS

Ambitions are sometimes just daydreams that never really materialize, and perhaps, if they do are seldom quite how we expected them to be, as this Chinese proverb indicates . . . 'Want a thing long enough and you don't'

'No bird soars too high if he soars with his own wings'

'He who leaps high must take a long run'
Danish

'He who would rise in the world should veil his ambition with the forms of humanity'
Chinese

'Who never climbed high never fell low'
English

'If you take big paces you leave big spaces'
Burmese

'Most people would succeed in small things, if they were not troubled with great ambitions'
Longfellow

'Who begins too much accomplishes little'
German

'We are all in the gutter, but some of us are looking at the stars . . .'
Oscar Wilde

FRIENDSHIP

It is good to meet old friends, but as many proverbs point out, it is possible to see too much of some of them. And to keep friendship green and healthy perhaps we should heed the French proverbial advice . . . 'A hedge between keeps friendship green'

'Your friend is the man who knows all about you, and still likes you'

'Life is partly what we make it, and partly what it is made by the friends whom we choose'
Chinese

'One loyal friend is worth ten thousand relatives'
Latin

'Thy friend has a friend, and thy friend's friend has a friend, so be discreet'
Talmud

'Better lose a jest than a friend'

'Many a friend was lost through a joke, but none was ever gained so'
Czech

'Friendship is a furrow in the sand'
Tongan

'Friends are lost by calling often and calling seldom'
French

'Visit your aunt, but not every day of the year'
Spanish

'One should go invited to a friend in good fortune, and uninvited in misfortune'
Swedish

'The constant friend is never welcome'
Yiddish

Mark Twain sums up friendship in a delightful way . . . 'The proper office of a friend is to side with you when you are in the wrong. Nearly anybody will side with you when you are in the right . . .'

FORTUNE

Some days everything seems to go well and we may say that 'Dame fortune is smiling upon us'. The superstitious among us insist that good luck needs to be fostered . . .

'When fortune knocks upon the door open it widely'
Spanish

'When fortune comes, seize her in the front with a sure hand, because behind she is bald'
Leonardo Da Vinci

'Fortune will call at the smiling gate'
Japanese

'Fortune's expensive smile is earned'

'Good luck beats early rising'
Irish

And a thought – making one from China . . .

'If luck comes, who comes not? If luck comes not, who comes?'

'Fortune is a woman; if you neglect her today do not expect to regain her tomorrow'
French

'A man does not seek his luck, luck seeks its man'
Turkish

'Luck is not chance; it's toil'

'Luck has a slender anchorage'
English

'Luck is loaned, not owned'

'When a man has luck, even his ox calves'
Yiddish

'Do not be born good or handsome, but be born lucky'
Russian

'Have but luck, and you will have the rest; be fortunate and
you will be thought great'
   Victor Hugo

'The lucky man's enemy dies, and the unlucky man's friend'
   Russian

'Fortune is blind, but not invisible'
   French

Probably very sound advice . . .
   'When ill luck falls asleep, let none wake her'
   Italian

SYMPATHY

Everybody needs sympathy from time to time. Some of these
proverbs sound rather cynical, but alas, sadly, many of them are
true . . .

'The comforter's head never aches'
   Italian

'When you live next to the cemetery you cannot weep for
everyone'
   Russian

'No man limps because another is hurt'
   Danish

'Nothing dries sooner than tears'
   Latin

'All things grow with time, except grief'
   Yiddish

'Search not the wound too deep, lest thou make a new one'
   Thomas Fuller

'Do not rejoice at my grief, for when mine is old, yours will
be new'
   Spanish

'When we sing everybody hears us, when we sigh nobody hears us'
Russian

SECRETS

'Another person's secret is like another person's money, you are not so careful with it as you are of your own'
Edgar Watson Howe

'To whom you tell your secrets, to him you resign your liberty'
Spanish

'Nothing is burdensome as a secret'
French

'Do not speak of secrets in a field that is full of little hills'
Hebrew

'A healthy ear can stand hearing sick words'
Senegalese

'Love, pain, and money cannot be kept secret; they soon betray themselves'
Spanish

'The secret of two no further will go, the secret of three a hundred will know'

'What belongs to everybody belongs to nobody'
Spanish

And someone once said . . . 'How can we expect another to keep our secret if we have been unable to keep it ourselves?'

BORROWING & LENDING

Borrowing and lending is universal, most days it crops up, and we all do so in good faith. Here is an old Indian proverb that is wise . . . 'What you loan out, you will never see again; or if you see it again then it will be decreased. Or if not decreased, then it will be different, or if not different, then you will have found an enemy'.

'Seldom a loan comes laughing home'

'A loan though old is no gift'
   Hungarian

'Eaten bread is soon forgotten'

likewise . . .
   'It is hard to pay for bread that has been eaten'
   Danish

'Money borrowed is soon sorrowed'

'Have a horse of your own and then you may borrow another's'
   Welsh

'Lend your money and lose your friend'
   English

'To lend is to buy a quarrel'
   Indian

'Better give a penny than lend twenty'
   Italian

And of lovers . . .
   'If you love him, don't lend him'
   Polish

'Only lend to a friend what you cannot afford to lose'
   Slovenian

'The law of lending is to break the dish'
   Irish

EXPERIENCE

If we went through life without gaining or learning by our various experiences, what a total waste it would be. And as Tennyson so aptly put it . . .

   'And other's follies teach us not,
   Nor much their wisdom teaches,

And most, of sterling worth, is what
Our own experience teaches'

'Only when you have crossed the river can you say the
crocodile has a lump on his snout'
  Ashanti

'Experience is a comb which nature gives us when we are bald'
  Chinese

'Only the wearer knows where the shoe pinches'
  English

'Experience is the only teacher, and we get his lesson
indifferently in any school'
  Emerson

'He who has once burnt his mouth always blows his soup'
  German

'I know by mine own pot how others boil'
  French

'Experience is good, if not bought too dear'
  English

'A piece of incense may be as large as the knee, but unless
burnt emits no fragrance'
  Malay

'He who has been bitten by a snake fears a piece of string'
  Persian

'*Experientia docet* — Experience teaches'

'Experience is not always the kindest of teachers, but it is
surely the best'
  Spanish

HONESTY

Long regarded as a virtue in many countries, it is a rarer thing
today perhaps. But one of the old Indian warrior tribes long ago

held another view. The hunter who could bring back the most prey, whether or not he had gleaned it from another hunter's snares, was the hero of the day. To be too honest was to show weakness, and weakness meant that such a man could therefore not be considered brave. Death was the solution for this offence if the 'weakness' continued — strange judgement indeed!

> 'He that resolves to deal with none but honest men must leave off dealings'
> *Thomas Fuller*

> 'A man who pursues honour, from him glory runs away'
> *The Talmud*

> 'The surest way to remain poor is to be an honest man'
> *French*

> 'Honest men marry soon, wise men not at all'

> 'Honesty is the best policy'
> *English*

'I have no idea what the mind of a lowlife scoundrel is like; but I know what the mind of an honest man is like. It is terrifying'
Abel Hermant

SILENCE

It has been said that silence goes hand in hand with wisdom; certainly it is not advantageous to tell everything that we may know:

> 'He is an ill companion that has a good memory'

> 'What one knows it is sometimes useful to forget'
> *Latin*

> 'Better say nothing, than nothing to the purpose'
> *English*

> 'A wise head makes a close mouth'

> 'Silence was never written down'
> *Italian*

'The silent dog is always the first to bite'
   German

'Many a man's tongue has broken his nose'

'We make more enemies by what we say than friends by what we do'
   Spanish

'It is best to sit near the chimney when the fire smokes'

'Talking pays no tolls'

'Silence is wisdom when speaking is folly'

'Silver silence is golden'
   English

'The stillest tongue can be the truest friend'

'Three silences there are; the first of speech,
'The second of desire, the third of thought'
   Longfellow

'Let a fool hold his tongue and he will pass for a sage'
   Latin

'It is better to conceal one's knowledge than to reveal one's ignorance'
   Spanish

From Mark Twain . . .
   'The right word may be effective, but no word was ever as effective as a rightly timed pause'

GRATITUDE

Gratitude is a debt which usually goes on accumulating like blackmail, the more you pay, the more is exacted . . .

'Next to ingratitude, the most painful thing to bear is gratitude'

'Gratefulness is the poor man's payment'
   English

'Revenge is profitable, gratitude is expensive'

'Ingratitude is a kind of weakness, clever men are not ungrateful'
French

'Gratitude is the memory of the heart'

HEALTH

To be healthy is something that is most essential if we are to succeed and achieve all our desires and ambitions . . .

'A healthy man is a successful man'
French

'The first wealth is health'

'Good health is above wealth'

'Your health comes first; you can always hang yourself later'
Yiddish

'Health is not valued till sickness comes'

'If you would live in health, be old early'
Spanish

'A little in the morning, nothing at noon, and a light supper doth make for a long life'

'He who was never sick dies of the first fit'
English

'Eat well, drink in moderation, and sleep sound,
In these three good health abound'
Latin

'Look to your health; and if you have it, praise God, and value it next to a good conscience; for health is the second blessing that we mortals are capable of. A blessing that money cannot buy . . .'
Izaac Walton

SLEEP

'Early to bed and early to rise,
Makes a man healthy, wealthy, and wise . . .'

'The net of the sleeper catches fish'
  Greek

'Take thy thoughts to bed with thee, for the morning is wiser than the evening'
  Russian

'Consult with your pillow'

'Night is the mother of counsel'
  Latin

'The best advice is found on the pillow'
  Danish

'He hath slept well, that remembers not he hath slept ill'
  Thomas Fuller

'Six hours' sleep for a man, seven for a woman and eight for a fool'
  English

'He that sleeps sound feels not the toothache'

'The night rinses what the day has soaped'
  Swiss

2
SAILORS, SHIPS AND LORE OF THE SEA

THE SEA HAS various names, affectionate or otherwise. To some it is known as the 'briny' or the 'hoggin,' to old sailors simply the 'andrew' or the 'drink,' but to most of us it is just 'the sea'. And the sea, as many famous writers and people have all said before me, has no generosity, no mercy on its victims, and indeed no quarter. Although most seafaring men all recognize this fact, I am sure it does not stop them from sailing and often pitting their strength against the full force of the sea and its inevitable moods.

Somebody once said . . . 'The sea is a hard master, and a cruel mistress'. For some reason, the sea and the ships that sail upon her are both thought of and spoken of as woman. Many attribute this fact to the age-old adage which holds that just as a woman is capricious and will go her own way, no matter the consequence, so does the sea.

'The sea is woman, the sea is wonderful,
Her other name is fate'

'Praise the sea but keep on land'

'A ship and a woman always want trimming'

'A sailor must have his eye trained to the rocks and sands as well as the north star'

'Call on God, but row away from the rocks'

'Ships fear fire more than water'

'A small leak will sink a great ship'

'While she creaks she holds'

'Every ship is a romantic object, except that we sail in'
Emerson

'Admire a little ship, but put your cargo in a big one'

'The sea has an enormous thirst and an insatiable appetite'
French

'Without oars, you cannot cross in a boat'
Japanese

'Too many boatmen will run the boat up to the top of the mountain'
Japanese

'In a calm sea every man is a pilot'
Spanish

A well-known saying uttered by many famous men and women is 'God bless this ship, and all who sail in her'. The custom of breaking a bottle of champagne, or wine, over the stem of a ship when launched originates from the old practice of drinking a toast of prosperity to the ship in a silver goblet. When drunk the goblet was cast into the sea, thus preventing another toast, perhaps of ill intent, being drunk from the same cup. The waste of silver goblets however resulted in another idea, simply breaking a bottle of wine over the stem. It was not until the Prince Regent decided, in 1811, to let women take part in this fine old tradition that the obvious need for a lanyard to secure the bottle to the ship was observed. Evidently too many spectators were getting hurt!

But one cannot help but feel, distressing though this fact might be, that it was infinitely better than one of the earliest customs observed. This involved the ritual murder of a young boy whose blood was offered as a blood sacrifice to the sea gods, and usually the blood would be liberally sprinkled over the deck of the vessel.

Sailors and seafaring men of all kinds are notoriously superstitious, and still to this day many of the old beliefs are still practised. It is thought unlucky to change the name of a ship . . . 'Change the name, change the luck'.

Whistling at sea is not a good omen; old sailors thought that whistling awoke the devil who would most likely send a storm to wreck the ship. Women and priests used not to be welcome passengers, and some animals were considered unlucky — cats (unless it was the ship's cat) goats, pigs and rabbits too. Here are some old nautical proverbs, some we all use often in everyday speech . . .

'Don't spoil the ship for a hap'orth 'o tar'

'Ships that pass in the night'

'Tell that to the Marines'

'Three sheets in the wind'

'Vows made in storms are forgotten in calms'
   French

'Once on shore we pray no more'

'Rats desert a sinking ship'

'To take the wind out of one's sails'

'A ship and a woman are ever repairing'
   Welsh

'Last ship, best ship'
   English

'Swinging the lead'

'I'm alright Jack!'

'A shot across the bows'

'Any port in a storm'

'Flogging a dead horse'

'Ship-shape and Bristol fashion'

'First turn of the screw pays all debts'

'Little fish is sweet'
'Worse things happen at sea'
   English

'Sling your hammock'

Fisherfolk, too, are usually mindful of ancient lore and legend as they still dislike to set sail on a Friday, and rarely like their womenfolk or family to wave them off on a fishing trip. Watching a boat disappear from view is thought to be an ill omen; it means for some families that the boat and its crew will never return. It is strange how these old customs can still persist even to this day.

Tides play an important part in every seaman's life, especially the fisherman . . .

'Time and tide wait for no man'
'Lose not a tide'

'There is a tide in the affairs of men,
Which, taken at the flood, leads on to fortune'
   Shakespeare

SEA-SICKNESS

It is an old sailor's proverb, that the only cure for sea-sickness is to sit on the shady side of an old brick church in the country.

'Sea-sickness is like dying several separate deaths'
English

'How unholy is sea-sickness, it robs one of all dignity!'

FISHING

Some proverbs about fishermen and the fish that try to elude them...

'The gods do not deduct from man's allotted span the hours spent in fishing'
Babylonian

'The best fish swims near the bottom'

'The end of fishing is not angling, but catching'
Turkish

'What baites one, banes another'
Scottish

'A thousand thousand knots,
A thousand thousand holes,'
— A fishing net
Yugoslav riddle

There's no catching trouts with dry breeches'
'The fish dies by its mouth'
Portuguese

'The fish will soon be caught that nibbles at every bait'

'Every fisher loves best the trout that is of his own tickling'
'It is ill fishing if the hook is bare'
   Scottish

'The fish may be caught in a net that will not come to the hook'

'However big the whale may be, the tiny harpoon can rob him of life'
   Malay

A quaint riddle from Sweden . . .
   'Who lives on the waves and makes his living from the wind?'
                                          — A fisherman

'When the fish is caught, the nets are laid aside'

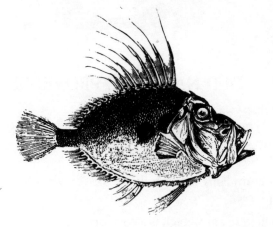

GULLS

And the gulls that screech and wheel around the shores of many countries, there are legends, sayings and proverbs about them also:

'If the gulls are out, good luck's about'

'No gulls, no luck'
   French

Seagulls in much earlier days, according to old superstition, were thought of as birds that embodied the souls of drowned or dead sailors everywhere, therefore it was very unlucky to kill one. If the gulls followed the fishing boats or other ships out to sea, then as the two old proverbs tell us, that was a good omen.

Nelson's flagship, HMS Victory, has an odd superstition about gulls. The gulls do not alight on the masts, rigging, or decks of the flagship, but it is noticeable that they settle quite naturally on other ships in the dockyard. Old sailors will tell you that the birds know that it was the ship in which Lord Nelson died.

OLD NAUTICAL PROVERBS

'He has swallowed the anchor'
'He who is shipwrecked the second time, cannot lay the blame on Neptune'
 English

'He complains wrongfully on the sea who twice suffers shipwreck'

'Society in shipwreck is a comfort to all'

'The sea refuses no river'
'The sea complains it wanteth water'

'Devil to pay and no pitch hot'

'Give a man a fish, and you feed him for a day. Teach a man to fish, and you feed him for a lifetime'
 Chinese

'No man cries stinking fish'
 English

'Two captains will sink the ship'
Turkish

'Like a fish out of water'
'I have other fish to fry'
Latin

'Scratch an Englishman, find a seaman'
English

JONAHS

The jinx sailor, or the 'Jonah' as he is often called is unwelcome on any ship, it has been known that should a ship discover a 'Jonah' then the rest of the crew would be tattooed at the next port of call! Tattooing could protect a sailor from the jinx if it took the form of a horse-shoe, or a four-leaf-clover, a rabbit's foot, or a black cat, and this would usually be done on the foot . . .

'He would sink a ship freighted with crucifixes'
French

'Pour gold on him, and he'll never thrive'

'He who is not lucky, let him not go to sea'
Latin

3
RICH MAN, POOR MAN, BEGGAR-MAN, THIEF

─────────────── RICH MAN ───────────────

'To be poor without murmuring is difficult. To be rich without being proud is easy'
  Confucius

'Riches serve a man, but command a fool'
  English

'To be rich is not everything, but it certainly helps'
  Yiddish

'In prosperity no altars smoke'
  Italian

'Poor men seek meat for their stomach, rich men stomach for their meat.'
  English

'It is better to live rich than to die rich'
  Samuel Johnson

'Much coin, much care'
  Latin

and likewise . . .
  'Small riches hath the most rest'
  Cornish

'Clogs to clogs in three generations'
  English

'Twice clogs, once boots'
'Rags to riches to rags'
  Lancastrian

Sadly a true fact; a fortune that may be amassed by one generation is squandered and thrown aside by the next. And as the old rhyme quoted tells us . . .

'Rags make paper,
Paper makes money,
Money makes banks,
Banks make loans,
Loans make beggars,
Beggars make rags'

'Riches are often abused, but never refused'

'Rich men have no faults'
Thomas Fuller

'With money you are a dragon; with no money, a worm'
Chinese

'Money draws money'
'Money begets money'

'Money never cometh out of season'
Old English

'The more one has, the more one wants'

'He is not fit for riches who is afraid to use them'

'Riches run after the rich, and poverty runs after the poor'
French

'The larger a man's roof the more snow it collects'
Persian

'Rich men feel misfortunes that fly over poor men's heads'

'He who is contented is not always rich'
Spanish

'Some people are masters of money, and some its slaves'
Russian

'The art is not in making money, but in keeping it'

'Penny and penny,
Laid up will be many,

Who will not save a penny,
Shall never have many'

'A penny saved is a penny gained'
  Scottish

Wise words from Francis Bacon . . . 1625 'Be not penny-wise;
riches have wings, and sometimes they fly away of themselves;
sometimes they must be set flying to bring in more'

'Riches certainly make themselves wings; they fly away as an
eagle towards heaven'
  Bible (Proverbs)

'It is easier for a camel to go through the eye of a needle, than
for a rich man to enter the kingdom of God'
  Bible

'He that is rich will not be called a fool'
  Spanish

'The longest road in the world is the one that leads to the
pocket'
'Sooner ask a man for his life, than for his money'
  Yiddish

'God help the rich, the poor can look after themselves'
'God help the rich man, let the poor man beg!'
  Old English

POOR MAN

'Poverty is no disgrace, but no honour either'
  Yiddish

'Poverty is no sin, but terribly inconvenient'
'The poor sleep soundly'
  Japanese

'Without money, without fear'

'Poverty is not perversity'
  Spanish

'Poor men's reasons are not heard'
  Thomas Fuller

'He who has no bread has no authority'
Turkish

'Wrinkled purses make wrinkled faces'
French

'An empty purse frightens away friends'
English

'To fry poverty, you need no butter'
Breton

'Lowly sit, richly warm'

'Do not spoil what you have by desiring what you have not; but remember that what you now have was once among the things only hoped for ...

'He is not poor that hath not much, but he that craves much'

'He is poor who does not feel content'
Japanese

'Bear wealth, poverty will bear itself'
French

'Remember that moderate riches will carry you; if you have more, you must carry them ...'
Anon

'Poor and contented is rich, and rich enough'
Shakespeare

'He is poor indeed that can promise nothing'

'A handsome man is not quite poor'
Spanish

'A poor man's roast and a rich man's death are sniffed far off'
Yiddish

'Better a little fire to warm us than a great one to burn us'
Thomas Fuller

'Poverty is very good in poems, but it is very bad in a house. It is very good in maxims and in sermons, but it is very bad in practical life . . .'
Henry Beecher Ward

BEGGAR-MAN

'Hark, Hark, the dogs do bark,
The beggars are coming to town,
Some in rags, and some in tags,
And some in velvet gown'

'Sit a beggar at your table and he will soon put his feet on it'
Russian

'Set a beggar on horseback and he'll ride at a gallop'

'Beggars mounted run their horses to death'

'Gifts make beggars bold'

'A beggar's purse is bottomless'

'Beggars breed and rich men feed'

'He that seeks alms for God's sake begs for two'

'He who beggeth for others is contriving for himself'

'The beggar is never out of his way'

'The beggar may sing before the thief'

'Small invitation will serve a beggar'

'One beggar at the door is enough'
'The poor man commands respect; the beggar must always excite anger'
French

'Beggars should be abolished entirely! Verily it is annoying to give to them, and it is annoying not to give to them.'
> *Nietzsche*

'It is better to be born a beggar than a fool'
> *Spanish*

'Beggars can never be bankrupts'
> *American*

'Beggars fear no rebellion'

'Beggars cannot be choosers'
> *English*

'Nothing agreeth worse,
Than a lady's heart and a beggar's purse'
> *John Heywood*

'One beggar does not hate another as much as one doctor hates another'
> *Polish*

THIEF

'A thief may pass for a gentleman when stealing has made him rich'

'An egg thief becomes a camel thief'
> *Persian*

'If you dip your arm into the picklepot let it be up to the elbow'
> *Malay*

'Opportunity makes the thief'
'One thief knows another'

'Set a thief to catch a thief'
English

'A thief believes everybody steals'

'Give a thief enough rope and he'll hang himself'

'God helps them that helps themselves'

And this old proverb surely must have given rise to this famous old Scottish epigram . . .

'He was a burglar stout and strong,
Who held, 'It surely can't be wrong,
To open trunks and rifle shelves,
For God helps those who help themselves.'
But when before the court he came,
And boldly rose to plead the same,
The judge replied, 'That's very true;
You've helped yourself, now God help you!'

'Save a thief from the gallows, and he will be the first to cut your throat'

'A man is not honest simply because he never had a chance to steal'
Yiddish

'Those who are once found to be bad are presumed to be so forever'
Latin

'Once a thief, always a thief'

'A thief is a hard master'

'There is honour even among thieves'
English

'To deny all, is to confess all'
Spanish

'Beauty provoketh thieves sooner than gold'
Shakespeare

'He who holds the ladder is as bad as the thief'
German

'The great thieves lead away the little thieves'
French

'A thief knows a thief as a wolf knows a wolf'

An old Malay proverb...
'Crime leaves a trail like a waterbeetle and like a snail it leaves its shine. Like a horse-mango it leaves its reek'

And now some proverbs concerning the other professions...

DOCTORS

Proverbs often provide sharp digs for the medical man, just as they do for other respected professions, sometimes dealing rather too unkindly, as will be noticed in some of the following...

'Many doctors, death accomplished'
Czech

'Better no doctor at all than three'
Polish

'Two doctors are better than one, but three doctors are fatal'
French

'A lucky physician is better than a learned one'
German

'A young doctor makes a humpy churchyard'
English

'A young doctor brings a green churchyard'
French

And likewise . . .

'Happy is the doctor who is called in at the decline of an illness'
Spanish

'The unlucky doctor treats the head of a disease, the lucky doctor its tail'
Chinese

'If you wish to die young, make your physician your heir'
Romanian

'Only a fool will make the doctor his heir'
Russian

'The doctor is often more to be feared than the disease'
French

'If the patient dies, the doctor has killed him, but if he gets well, the saints have saved him'
Italian

'If the doctor cures the sun sees it, but if he kills the earth hides it'
French

And from Molière . . .
'There's a sort of decency among the dead, a remarkable discretion, you never find them making any complaint against the doctor who killed them!'

'Every physician almost hath his own favourite disease'
Henry Fielding

'There is no better surgeon than one with many scars'
Spanish

'The best surgeon is he that hath been hacked himself'
'Physicians faults are covered with earth, and rich men's money'
English

'Study sickness while you are well'
Thomas Fuller

'Patience is the best medicine'

'By medicine life may be prolonged, yet death may seize the doctor too!'
   Shakespeare

'He who conceals his disease cannot expect to be cured'
   Ethiopian

'There are more old drunkards than old doctors'
   French

'Physicians are costly visitors'

'Sickness soaks the purse'

'God heals, and the physician takes the fee'
   French

'A physician is an angel when employed, but a devil when one must pay him'
   Latin

'If you despise the doctor, also despise the disease'
   Bantu

And from an Indian doctor...
   'I have lanced many boils, but none pained like my own'

LAWYERS

Just as the physician receives short shrift from many countries so does the lawyer. Many are the hidden barbs and many are the proverbs often quoted!

'God wanted to chastise mankind, so he sent lawyers'
   Russian

'One lawyer will make work for another'
   Spanish

'A lawyer never goes to law himself'
   English

'If there were no bad people there would be no good lawyers'
   Charles Dickens

'Lawyers' houses are built on the heads of fools'

41

'The devil makes his Christmas-pie of lawyers' tongues and clerks' fingers'

'It usually takes a hundred years to make a law, and then, after it has done its work, it usually takes a hundred years to get rid of it.'
Henry Beecher Ward

'Law cannot punish where it cannot persuade'

'Everyone loves justice in the affairs of another'
Italian

'Two attorneys can live in a town, where one cannot'

'God works wonders now and then;
Behold! a lawyer, an honest man!'
Benjamin Franklin

'He that loves law will get his fill of it'
Scottish

'The bare right is almost injustice'
Irish

'The robes of lawyers are lined with obstinacy of suitors'
Italian

'In law there's many a loss without a gain, but never a gain without a loss'

'Injustice all round is justice!'
Persian

'A good lawyer makes a bad neighbour'

'A lean compromise is better than a fat lawsuit'

'Agree! for the law is costly!'

Samuel Butler once said . . . 'A lawyer's dream of heaven. Every man reclaimed his property on resurrection, and each tried to recover it from all his forefathers'

PRIESTS

'A broad hat does not always cover a venerable head'

'He who is near the church is often far from God'
French

'Tis not the habit that makes the monk'
Fuller

'Hood an ass with reverend purple so you can hide his two ambitious ears, and he shall pass for a cathedral doctor'
Ben Jonson

'The devil gets up to the belfry by the vicar's skirts'
Thomas Fuller

'There are three sexes; men, women, and clergymen'
Sydney Smith

'Many come to church to air their finery'
French

'Many come to bring their clothes to church rather than themselves'
Thomas Fuller

Here is an old rhyme which may be of Scottish origin . . .

'I cannot praise the Preacher's eyes,
    I never saw his glance divine,
He always shuts them when he prays,
    And when he preaches he shuts mine'

'They are not all saints who use holy waters'
English

'The painful preacher, like a candle bright, consumes himself in giving others light'
Benjamin Franklin

'In the visible church the true Christians are invisible'
German

'A man does not have to attend church to be a Christian'
English

'Some go to church to see and be seen,
Some go there to say they have been,
Some go there to sleep and nod,
But few go there to worship God'

'The preacher's garment is cut according to the pattern of that of the hearers, for the most part!'
Oliver Wendell Holmes

'There are many preachers who don't hear themselves'
German

'God will listen to you whatever cloak you wear'
Spanish

POLITICIANS

'A man ain't got no right to be a public man, unless he meets the public'
Charles Dickens

'It is terrible to speak well and be wrong!'
Sophocles

'Politicians are like weather vanes'
French

'To be a public man is slavery'
American

POETS

'Poets and painters have leave to lie'

'Poetry is the mirror of the soul'
English

'Would you be a poet before you've been to school?
Ah, well I hardly thought you,
So absolute a fool.'
Lewis Carroll

'A good poet's made as well as born'

'A very good or very bad poet is remarkable; but a middling
one who can bear?'
Thomas Fuller

'The verse will halt if the tongue's too true'
Burmese

'Poets are born, but orators are made'

TEACHERS

'A teacher is better than two books'
German

'To teach is to learn twice over'

'If a man keeps cherishing his old knowledge so as continually to
be acquiring new, he may be a teacher of others'
Confucius

'A teacher stands in fear of teaching'
French

'Learning without thought is labour lost'
Confucius

'He teacheth ill, who teacheth all'
English

'Whom God teaches, man cannot'

'Experience is the only teacher'

'There are no national frontiers to learning'
Japanese

'It is safer to learn than to teach; and who conceals his opinion has nothing to answer for'
William Penn

'A little learning is a dangerous thing'

'Knowledge, teaching and words may be deeds'
Spanish

SERVANTS

'The noblest service comes from nameless hands,
And the best servant does his work unseen'
Oliver Wendell Holmes

'If you pay not a servant his wages then he will pay himself'
Spanish

'He that would be well served must know when to change his servants.'

'If the servant grows rich and the master poor, they are both good for nothing'
German

'A good servant makes a bad enemy'
English

'They also serve who only stand and wait'
John Milton

'He too serves a certain purpose who only stands and cheers'

'He who serves two masters has to lie to one'
Portuguese

'No man can serve two masters'
Bible

'If you want good service, serve yourself'
Spanish

'If you want a thing done well, do it yourself'
Napoleon

'Servants like ornaments should be used in their proper places'
English

KINGS

'Uneasy lies the head that bears the crown'
Shakespeare

'The royal crown cures not the headache'

'Kings are like stars they rise and set,
They have the worship of the world, but no repose . . .'
Shelley

'High birth is a poor dish at table'
Italian

'A man who prides himself on his ancestry is like the potato plant, the best part of which is underground'
Spanish

'Noble and common blood is of the same colour'
German

'A throne is only a bench covered with velvet'
French

'Look down if you would know how high you stand'
Yiddish

'He that eats of the king's goose shall be choked with feathers'
English

'King's venison is sooner eaten than digested'
Dorset

'The King's cheese goes half-way in parings'

'Better in the dust than crawl near the throne'
German

'Nearest the king, nearest the gallows'

'A king's favour is no inheritance'

'He who would rule must hear and be deaf, see and be blind'
German

'A good mind possesses a kingdom'

'Only with a new ruler do you realise the value of the old'
Burmese

'What are kings, when regiment is gone,
But perfect shadows in a sunshine day'
Christopher Marlowe

ACTORS

'He who would climb the ladder must begin at the bottom'
English

'A minute's success pays the failure of years'
Robert Browning

'There are many paths to the top of the mountain, but the view is always the same'
Chinese

'Fame is a magnifying glass'
English

'Blessed is he whose fame does not outshine his truth'

'Fame is a constant effort'

'Fame usually comes to those who are thinking about something else'
Oliver Wendell Holmes

'The top of a pinnacle now, firewood soon'
Burmese

'If the audience never understands the plot, it can be counted on to be attentive to the very end' . . . wise words from Benedetto Marcello as long ago as 1720.

ARTISTS

'One picture in ten thousand, perhaps, ought to live in the applause of mankind, from generation to generation, until the colours fade and blacken out of sight or the canvas rot entirely away'
Nathaniel Hawthorn

'Knowledge without practice makes but half the artist'

'Art helps nature, and experience art'

'Art lies in concealing art'
'Art has no enemy except ignorance'
Latin

'An artist is at home everywhere'

'A good artist can draw a devil as well as an angel'

'To whiten ivory with dye is to spoil nature by art'
Latin

'In art, as in love, instinct is enough'

TAILORS

'Good clothes open all doors'

'Fine feathers make fine birds'
English

'Those who have fine clothes in their chests can wear rags'
Italian

'Clothes and manners do not make the man; but when he is made they greatly improve his appearance'
Henry Beecher Ward

'There's never a new fashion but it's old'

'The present fashion is always handsome'
Thomas Fuller

'Fashion is more powerful than any tyrant'
Latin

'In clothes as well as speech, the man of sense,
Will shun all these extremes that give offense,
Dress unaffectedly, and, without haste,
    Follow the changes in the current taste.'
Molière

'Tailors and writers must mind the fashion'
English

'Nine tailors maketh a man'

'He that doth not rob makes not a robe or garment'
Spanish

'A hundred tailors, a hundred weavers, and a hundred millers make three hundred thieves'

'Let me be dressed fine as I will,
Flies, worms, and flowers, exceed me still'
Isaac Watts

FOOLS OR JESTERS

'Wit is never good till it be bought'

'To be a fool at the right time is also an art'

'He who lives without folly is not so wise as he thinks'

'He is a fool who looks for a notch in a saw'
Yiddish

'If you be a jester, keep your wit till you have use for it'
Latin

'There is no fool like an old fool'

'Send a fool to the market, and a fool he'll return'
English

'He is a fool that is not melancholy once a day'
Latin

'The fool wanders, the wise man travels'

'A fool and his money are soon spent'

'Experience keeps a dear school, but fools will learn in no other'

'He is not a wise man who cannot play the fool on occasions'

'An hour of play discovers more than a year of conversation'
Portuguese

'Mingle just a little folly with your wisdom'
French

'Let us be thankful for the fools. But for them the rest of us could not succeed . . .'
Mark Twain

'If every fool wore a crown, we should all be kings'
Welsh

'There is no need to fasten a bell to a fool'
Danish

'There are bearded fools'
English

'A fool's head never whitens'
English

'A learned fool is sillier than an ignorant one'
Molière

'If the fools do not control the world, it isn't because they are not in the majority.'
Edgar Watson Howe

'There are four types of men in the world; lovers, opportunists, lookers-on, and imbeciles. The happiest are the imbeciles.'

MUSICIANS

Of music and musicians . . .

'Who hears music feels his solitude'

'Music hath charms to soothe a savage breast'

'Where there's music there can be love'
French

'In a fiddler's house all are dancers'

'Music is ever sweetest at the close'

'And the night shall be filled with music
And the cares that infest the day,
Shall fold their tents like the Arabs,
And as silently steal away . . .'
Longfellow

'There are harps in heaven, but cymbals in hell'
Irish

HARLOTS

'The love of a harlot and wine of a flagon, are good in the morning but naught in the evening'

'Whoredom and grace ne'er dwelt in one place'
'There is no need of a ferret to catch a harlot'
'A woman that loves to be at the window is a bunch of grapes on the highway'
English

'Love makes the time pass. Time makes love pass'

'Life is never long enough for a coquette'
French

'A mistress in a high place is not a bad thing'
Spanish

WRITERS

'The pen is mightier than the sword'

'Some men have only one book in them, others a library'

'A wicked book is the wickeder because it cannot repent'
English

'There is much good sleep in an old story'
German

'Books and friends should be few and good'

The difficulty of literature is not to write, but to write what you mean'
Robert Louis Stevenson

'Writing comes more easily if you have something to say'

'The secret of all good writing is sound judgement'

'An honest tale speeds best being plainly told'
Shakespeare

'There are several kinds of stories, but only one difficult kind — the humorous . . .'
Mark Twain

53

4

GARDEN-LORE, TREES AND FLORA

THE GARDEN IS still a place full of much mystical and superstitious lore. The art of growing things practised by the owners of those much envied 'green fingers' remains even today. When one considers that plants, flowers and trees were, in the not-so-distant past, thought to be the homes of elemental spirits, or of fairies, both good and bad, who would greatly influence the success or failure of the garden, one is not really surprised to find today many small bearded gnomes in residence.

Perhaps these small, active little creatures, sometimes busily fishing or hoeing, have taken over as our modern guardians, keeping up the old belief of having the little folk dwelling in our gardens to see that all is well. Naturally many of the old superstitions and garden-lore still live on in numerous proverbs.

——— TREES ———

'He that plants trees loves others besides himself'
English

'Large trees give more shade than fruit'

'Great trees keep little ones down'
American

'Trees often transplanted seldom prosper'
Dutch

'The tree casts its shade upon all, even the woodcutter'
Hindu

A very old riddle . . .
    'In spring I delight you,
    In summer I cool you,
    In autumn I feed you,
    In winter I warm you'
       — A tree

'The forest is the poor man's overcoat'
    American

'A forest is in an acorn'
    Anon

'When an oak tree is felled, the whole forest echoes with it, but a hundred acorns are planted silently by some unseen force'
    Thomas Carlyle

'If you cut down the trees you will find the wolf'
    American

'When a dead tree falls, the woodpeckers share in its death'
    Malay

'The fall of a leaf is a whisper to the living'
    English

'A tree falls the way it leans'
    Bulgarian

'Though a tree grow ever so high, the falling leaves return to the root'
    Malay

'Plant a poplar and sigh forever'

A strange old custom was observed with the planting of poplar trees in many country places. As the tree always seemed to sigh with the wind it was thought of as 'the sad tree' so at lamb-docking time, a tail would be planted under each newly planted poplar tree to keep sorrow away from the house and family.

There are also many wise sayings connected with fruit trees. Charles Dickens had this thought about fig trees . . .

'Train a fig-tree in the way it should go, and when you are old sit under the shade of it'

'Peel a fig for your friend, a peach for your enemy'

'If you would enjoy the fruit, pluck not the flower'

'Plant the crab tree where you will and it will never bear pippins'

'There is small choice in rotten apples'

'If good apples you would have, the leaves must go to the grave'

'Apples taste sweetest when they are going'
    Latin

'Your neighbour's apples are the sweetest'
    Yiddish

'He that would have the fruit must climb the tree'
    Thomas Fuller

'It is only at the tree loaded with fruit that the people throw stones'
    French

'Till St Swithin's day be past,
The apples be not fit to taste'

'Better is one apple given than two eaten'

'Apples, pears, and nuts spoil the voice'

'An apple a day keeps the doctor away'

When old fruit trees are felled to clear land, frequently old coins are found buried among their roots, or perhaps small pieces of coal.

These discoveries suggest that the old primitive belief of making a small sacrifice to the trees was ever prevalent, this was the way the ancient folk ensured themselves and their families of a plentiful bumper crop.

'Plant pears for your heirs'

'After pear, wine or the priest'

'A pear must be eaten to the day; if you don't eat it then, throw it away!'

'No pear falls into a shut mouth'
   Italian

This proverb, I feel, is echoed in some logic gathered from the Argentine . . . 'A man was sleeping under a pear tree, when suddenly a snake came. A pear fell waking him. He killed the snake and ate the pear.'

'If cherries blow in April, you'll have your fill; but if in May they'll go away'

'A cherry year, a merry year;
A plum year, a dumb year;
A pear year, a dear'

'A black plum is as sweet as a white'

'In the year when plums flourish, all else fails'
   English

And more trees . . .
   'He who plants a walnut tree expects not to eat of the fruit'

'A woman, a steak, and a walnut tree, the more they are beaten the better they be'
   Italian

'When the elder is white, brew and bake a peck,
When the elder is black, brew and bake a sack'

Even today there are people who regard the elder as a sacred tree, and nothing would make them cut down or destroy an elder, believing there is an age-old curse for the person that does so, which means death or misfortune for the immediate family. This old belief originates from the apostle Judas who was said to have hanged himself on a cross made from an elder tree. Those who gather firewood will avoid elder, to burn it is 'to raise the devil!'

'You may shear your sheep,
When the elder blossoms peep'

'Deeds are fruits, words are leaves'
    English

'When all fruit fails, welcome haws'
    Scottish

'By their fruits ye shall know them'
    Bible

'Set trees poor and they grow rich; set them rich and they oft grow poor'
    English

GARDEN-LORE

'Every garden may have some weeds'
    English

'As is the gardener, so is the garden'

'A garden requireth three things, fair weather, a good feed, and a good gardener'

'The bad gardener quarrels with his rake'
    American

'Tis the gardener's care that makes a plot bear'

'A prudent man does not make the goat his gardener'
    Hungarian

'Some people like to make of life a garden, and to walk only within its paths'
    Japanese

'God the first garden made, and the first city Cain'
    English

There are many old superstitions about garden flowers — some pleasant, others rather melancholy. These come, I am certain, from the old pagan beliefs that flowers were the homes for the souls of the dead. Since then much of the old lore has been handed on to us so that the superstitious among us still hesitate when tempted to cut certain flowers and bring them into the house. Lilac is looked upon as a sign of illness; delicate mimosa brings a death; snowdrops and daffodils, too, are not considered by some as 'lucky' flowers. May flowers are really the unluckiest of all, and for this there is a good enough reason. In pagan times the unfortunates intended for human sacrifice were always first crowned with wreaths of may blossom.

'Keep may out, keep death out'
Old English

'A flower cannot blossom without sunshine, nor a garden without love'

'Many eyes go through the meadow, but few see the flowers'
English

'Pleasures are like poppies spread;
You seize the flow'r, its bloom is shed'
Robert Burns

'One flower will not make a garland'
French

ROSES

'A rose too often smelled loses its fragrance'
Spanish

'Anything may be spoken if it be under the rose'
Old English

'He who wants a rose must respect the thorn'
Persian

'When the roses are gone, nothing is left but the thorn'
  Ovid

'Gather ye rosebuds while ye may,
Old time is still a flying,
And this same flower that smiles today,
Tomorrow will be dying'
  Robert Herrick

'He that plants thorns must never expect to gather roses'
  English

'He that scattereth thorns must not go barefoot'

WEEDS

One of the prettiest little weeds I know is the Scarlet Pimpernel, known to country people everywhere as 'the poor man's weather glass'. It is a very reliable forecaster of sun or rain, if open wide then you can expect it to stay fine for an hour or so, but if closed then rain is on the way.

The old pimpernel rhyme . . .
  'Pimpernel, pimpernel tell me true,
  Whether the weather be fine or true,
  No heart can think,
  No tongue can tell,
  The virtues of the pimpernel'

NETTLES

'Nettles don't sting in the month of May'
  English

'Nettles are never frostbitten'
Slovenian

'He that handles a nettle tenderly is soonest stung'
English

'Tender handed stroke a nettle,
And it stings you for your pains,
Grasp it like a man of mettle,
And it soft as silk remains'
Aaron Hill

THISTLES

'He that sows thistles shall reap prickles'

'A thistle is a fat salad for an ass's mouth'
Scottish

'Cut thistles in May,
They grow in a day,
Cut them in June,
That is too soon,
Cut in July,
Then they will die'

'They have need of a blessing that kneel to a thistle'

'A weed is no more than a flower in disguise,
Which is seen through at once, if love give a man eyes'

HERBS

'Sow fennel, sow trouble'
'Rue only flourishes if it be stolen'
English

Rosemary . . . Sir Thomas More said of rosemary . . . 'I lette it runne all over my garden walls, not onlie because the bees love it, but because it is the herb of friendship, whence a sprig of it hath a dumb language'

'Rosemary flourishes where the wife rules'

'Where rosemary grows the wife wears the trousers'
French

(This fragrant herb when once well established will live for thirty three years, the traditional age of Christ, and then will grow no taller.)

> 'If the sage-bush thrives and grows,
> The master's not master, and he knows'

> 'Parsley won't grow where the mistress is master'

> 'The herb that can't be got is the one that heals'
> *Irish*

> 'Garlic by the savour, bread by the colour'
> *French*

Grass
> 'Grass never grows where the wind blows'

> 'If the grass grows in January, it grows the worse for all the year'

> 'Grass never grows on a busy street'

> 'The grass is always greener on the other side of the fence'

NATURE

> 'Wherever Nature does least, man does most'

> 'He that followeth Nature is never out of his way'

> 'Nature goes her own way'
> *English*

'In Nature, Time and Patience are the three great physicians'

'Accuse not Nature! she hath done her part,
Do thou but thine'
  John Milton

'Nature takes as much pains in the forming of a tree as she does an emperor'

'The book of Nature is the book of Fate. She turns the gigantic pages — leaf after leaf, never returning one'
  Emerson

'One touch of nature makes the whole world kin'
  Shakespeare

'Nature is the art of God'
  Dante

5

WEATHER-LORE AND COUNTRY SAYINGS

THROUGHOUT THE CENTURIES all over the world people have always been very concerned about the weather, and have watched for signs and happenings in nature to guide them about their daily work. Country folk, farmers in particular, had much to lose if crops did not prosper so they chose their sowing days with great care. Generally saints' days and holy days were considered to be the best choice. And this could well be where the old proverb 'The better the day, the better the deed' originated.

Candlemas day, the second day of February, was an important day in the old country year as this ancient rhyme tells . . .

> 'If Candlemas Day be warm and bright,
> Winter will take another bite,
> But if Candlemas Day brings cold and rain,
> Winter is gone, and won't come again'

And another old rhyming proverb . . .
> 'A farmer should on Candlemas Day,
> Have half his corn and half his hay'

Many favoured Good Friday for the first sowing of peas, beans and potatoes, and if it rained on Good Friday this old proverb was observed with delight . . .
> 'Rain on Good Friday foretells a fruitful year'
and . . .
> 'A good deal of rain upon Easter Day gives a
> crop of good grass, but little good hay'

When the sowing did begin in earnest the farmer and his workers were especially careful 'not to miss a bout'. This meant not missing a line in the field when sowing. If this happened it meant that someone belonging to the farm would die before reaping.

This old rhyme was often sung by the children whilst the sowing was in process . . .

'One to rot and one to grow,
One for the pigeon, one for the crow'

Another rhyme heeded by country folk everywhere as they looked anxiously at the trees each year . . .

'If the oak is out before the ash,
Then we are going to have a splash,
But if the ash is out before the oak,
Summer will be just one long soak'

Other countries also took notice of the trees and the swelling buds. The old American Indians said that when the leaves of the fragrant osage orange, the whitebeam and the hickory were as fat as a squirrel's ear, then it was time to sow corn. The early settlers in the colonies very naturally took many old beliefs and superstitions with them and proverbs too. So that variations on many a well-known saying and proverb must have come about in this way.

RAIN

Many rain proverbs have a similarity . . .
'Rain from the east, two wet days at least'

'A sunshiny shower won't last half an hour'

'Rain before seven, clear before eleven'

'When the dew is on the grass,
Rain will never come to pass'

'A dry lent, a fertile year'
Scottish

'Before St John's Day (24th June) for rain we pray, after that we get it anyway'
English

Perhaps one of the best known weather proverbs in rhyme . . .

'St Swithin's Day, if thou be fair,
For forty days 'twill rain no more,
St Swithin's Day, if thou bring rain,
For forty days it will remain'

The old legend of St Swithin, who was Bishop of Winchester (A.D. 800-862) tells us that when he lay dying one of his last wishes was to be buried simply in the churchyard, so that the rain would fall on him and the feet of the ordinary people that he had loved so well would pass over his head. His wishes were carried out, he was buried in the cathedral yard, and it was not until many years later that the Winchester monks began to be rather concerned about the saint's lowly grave, and decided to remove his remains and re-bury them within the cathedral. They began the removal on July 15th, but the rain fell in such torrents that work had to be postponed. The heavy rains continued for forty days and nights, so that the monks became uneasy and people said that the saint was displeased and that this was his way of showing his displeasure. Finally the idea was abandoned, St Swithin was left as he had wished in common ground, a small chapel was built over the grave, thus making it into a little shrine for the people to come and worship there.

A few more rain proverbs . . .

'The rain does not fall on one roof alone'
Cameroonian

'The good rain, like a preacher does not know when to stop'

'Although it may rain, cast not away the watering pot'
Malay

'Bad weather is always worse through a window'

'A dry May and a dripping June,
Bringeth all things into tune'

and . . .

'Calm weather in June sets the corn in tune'
American

'A leaky May and a June,
Brings on the harvest very soon'

'A drowning man is not troubled by rain'
Persian

'The highest flood has the lowest ebb'

CLOUDS

'When clouds appear
Like rocks and towers
The earth's refreshed
By frequent showers'

'Every cloud has a silver lining'
English

'Clouds gather before a storm'

'One cloud is enough to eclipse all the sun'

'Every cloud engenders not a storm'
Shakespeare

'He that observeth the wind shall not sow; and he that
regardeth the clouds shall not reap'
Bible

'Mackerel sky,
Mackerel sky,
Not long wet
And not long dry'

RAINBOWS

The Old Norsemen used to call the rainbow 'the bridge of the
Gods' and Noah looked upon it as a sign that God would never

flood the world again. Old folklore and superstition say that at the end of the rainbow there is a crock of gold, a charming old legend holds that every time a rainbow appears in an evening sky we may wish once, and that wish will surely be granted.

An old Chinese proverb in rhyme . . .
> 'A rainbow in the Eastern sky,
> The morrow will be fine and dry.
> A rainbow in the West that gleams,
> Rain tomorrow falls in streams'

> 'Rainbow at noon, rain comes soon'
> *English*

> 'Rainbow at morn,
> Put your hook in the corn,
> Rainbow at eve,
> Put your head in the sheave'

WIND

> 'The devil is busy in a high wind'

> 'God tempers the wind to the shorn lamb'

> 'A little wind kindles, too much puts out the fire'

> 'A windy Christmas and calm Candlemas are signs of a good year'

> 'The wind keeps not always in one quarter'

> 'It is an ill wind that blows nobody any good'

> 'No weather is ill if the wind be still'

> 'A blustering night, a fair day follows'
> *Spanish*

From Poland this charming old riddle . . .
> 'I have neither body nor soul, but when I play on my flute everything starts to dance. What am I?
> — The wind

> 'Many can brook the weather that love not the wind'
> *Shakespeare*

'A dry east wind raises the spring'
Cornish

'When the wind's in the east on Candlemas Day, there it will stick till the end of May'

'When the wind is in the east,
Tis neither good for man nor beast,
When the wind is in the north,
The skilful fisher goes not forth;
When the wind is in the south,
It blows the bait in the fishes mouth,
But when the wind is in the west,
Then 'tis at its very best . . .'

THUNDER AND STORMS

As these can both occur at any time it seems, naturally there are many sayings and proverbs about them . . .

'A winter thunder, a summer's wonder'

'Thunder is the devil's wrath'

'Early thunder, early spring'

'Thunder in spring, cold will bring'

'Autumn thunder, means a mild winter'
Norwegian

'They sicken of the calm, who know the storm'

'The whispering grove tells of a storm to come'
Hampshire

'A fair day in winter is the mother of a storm'
English

'The day of the storm is not the time for thatching'
Irish

'After a storm comes a calm'

'When trout refuse bait or fly,
Storm it is that now is nigh'

'Red sky at night,
Shepherd's delight;
Red sky in the morning;
Shepherd's warning'

THE MOON

The different phases of the moon were always very important to the countryman and the farmer. Even today in our modern society it is still thought by many that the moon is responsible for strange behaviour in some people. The sight of a new moon in the sky, just a slim silver sickle is still enough in many parts of the world to set folks bobbing a courtsey or making a bow in homage, and then often turning their money over. The moon's phases were consulted from old almanacs for sowing, reaping and planting. Seed sown when the moon's rays were increasing meant that they grew with the moon, and this was considered to be sound and practical.

'Don't plant seed too soon, consult the moon'

'A ring around the moon, rain comes soon'

'Should the moon rise haloed round,
Soon we'll walk on deluged ground'

'An old moon in a mist is worth gold in the chest,
But a new moon and a mist, we'll never lack water'

'In the waning of the moon, cloudy morn, fair afternoon'

'When the moon is not full, the stars shine more brightly'
Bugandan

'When the moon lies on her back,
Then the sou'west wind will crack,
When she rises up and nods,
Chill nor'easters dry the sods.'

'A Saturday moon, if it comes once in seven years, it comes too soon'

An old moon riddle...
'There is a thing 'twas three weeks old
When Adam was no more,
This thing it was but four weeks old
When Adam was four score...'

'A full moon eats clouds'

'When a finger points at the moon, the imbecile looks at the finger'
Chinese

'The man in the moon was caught in a trap,
For stealing the thorns from another man's gap,
If he had gone by, and let the thorns lie,
He'd never been man in the moon so high...'

THE SUN

People of many nations have worshipped the sun. Early civilisations believed that spirits lived in the sun, moon and stars. The great sun god was feared and many sacrifices were made to keep him happy. The ancient Druids who worshipped the sun were reputed to make human sacrifices on Midsummer Eve. At this time of year the power of the sun noticeably decreased and to ancient folks this was a sign that the great sun god was displeased, so they lit huge fires, made sacrifices of animals, birds and fish, all in a vain attempt to boost and cheer their despondent god...

'The morning sun never lasts the day'

'The sun will set without thy assistance'
Hebrew

71

'Make hay while the sun shines'
English

'Although the sun shine, leave not thy cloak at home'

'He that hath a head of wax must not walk in the sun'
Latin

'Stars are not seen by sunshine'
Spanish

'If the sun shines while it rains, the devil is beating his mother'
Greek

An old rhyming riddle for the sun from Spain . . .
'As red as an apple,
As round as a ball,
Higher than the steeple,
Weathercock and all . . .'

'It is not necessary to light a candle to the sun'
Chinese

'With so many roosters crowing, the sun never comes up'
Italian

'The sun, though it passes through dirty places, yet remains as pure as before . . .'
Francis Bacon

MISTS AND FOGS

Fog which often shrouds a town or the countryside used to have a special meaning in earlier days. It was thought that the Devil and his legions were up to no good, and needed the mists and fogs to hide their evil deeds. Not everyone, however, thought like that in later years; here is a fisherman's version . . .
'When the mist creeps up the hill,
Fisherman out and try your skill,
When the mist begins to nod,
Fisherman then put up your rod . . .'

'A fog and a small moon bring an easterly wind soon'
Cornish

'A fog from the sea brings corn to the mills'
English

'So many fogs in March, so many frosts in May'

'A summer fog is for fair weather'

'Fog on the hill,
Water for the mill,
Fog in the hollow;
A fine day will follow'

——WEATHER & THE ANIMAL KINGDOM ——

The old countryman thought as much about his animals and livestock as about his crops. He took particular notice of their habits and often attributed them to the various quirks of the weather. Here is a selection of old animal and bird proverbs, some in rhyme, many of which you may find amusing. Most of them are very old and suprisingly quite often true!

'If the cock crows before he goes to bed,
He's sure to rise with a watery head'

'When sheep and lambs do gambol and fight,
The weather will change before the night'

'When the peacock loudly calls, then look out for storms and squalls'

'Harry no man's cattle'

'If the birds whistle in January there are frosts to come'

'When plovers do fast appear,
It shows that frosts are very near,
But when the plovers thus do go,
Then you may look for heavy snow.'

'Spider's webs floating at an autumn sunset bring a night frost'

'When the glow-worm lights her lamp, the air is always very damp'
Georgia

73

'When you see gossamer flying, be sure the air is drying'
Florida

'When eager bites the thirsty flea, clouds and rain you'll surely see'

'When harvest flies hum, there's warm weather to come'
English

'When a cow tries to scratch its ear,
It means a shower be very near,
When it begins to thump its rib with its tail,
Look out for thunder, lightning and hail'
Old English

'The jay bird don't rob his own nest'
West Indies

'Bees will not swarm before a near storm'

'If the bees stay at home, rain will come soon,
If they fly away, then fine is the day'

'A swarm of bees in May,
Is worth a load of hay,
A swarm of bees in June
Is worth a silver spoon,
But a swarm in July,
Is not worth a fly...'

'When you hear the asses bray,
We shall have rain on that day'

'It does not always rain when the pig squeals'
    American

'When pigs carry sticks,
The clouds will play tricks,
When they lie in the mud,
No fear of a flood'

'After a famine in the stall,
Comes a famine in the hall'

'If the adder could hear
And the blind worm could see
Neither man nor beast
Would ever go free . . .'

'When the blackbird sings before Christmas she will cry at
Candlemas'

'If the robin sings in the bush,
Then the weather will be coarse,
If the robin sings in the barn;
The weather will be warm . . .'

——— SEASONAL & COUNTRY ———

Some more countryman's proverbs gathered from many different
parts of the world, some are very similar, others contradictory . . .

'A late Easter, a long cold spring'
    French

'A good bark year makes a good wheat year'
    Indian

'Every mile in winter is two'
'For a morning's rain leave not your journey'
'The first and last frosts are the worst'
    English

'A great dowry is a bed of brambles'
'A bad farmers's hedge is full of gaps'
'A lazy reaper never gets a good sickle'
    Welsh

'Where everyone goes, the grass never grows'
   Irish

'Cursing the weather is never good farming'
   Cheshire

'The best manure is under the farmer's foot'
'An ill workman always blames his tools'
   English

'A wet May was never kind yet'
   French

'A dry May and a leaking June makes the farmer whistle a merry tune'
   Isle of Man

'A dry summer never made a dear peck'
   Somerset

'Hunger find no fault with mouldy corn'
   Massachusetts

'Measure the corn of others with your own bushel'
   Yiddish

'A mill cannot grind with water that is past'
   Rhode Island

'You cannot drive a windmill with a pair of bellows'
   Connecticut

'Good weight and measure are heaven's treasure'
   American

'Under the mountains is silver and gold,
But under the night sky, hunger and cold'
   Indian

'A bad bush is better than an open field'
   French

'He that has a good harvest must be content with a few thistles'
   Spanish

'While one milks the ram, the other holds under the sieve'
Chinese

'What the rake gathers, the fork scatters'
Russian

WINTER

And now to winter's blast . . .
'The melancholy days are come, the saddest of the year, of wailing winds, and naked woods and meadows brown and sear . . .'
William Cullen Bryant

Winter shall find what summer has left'

'Winter weather and women's thoughts soon change'

'When November's ice will bear a duck,
Winter will be all slosh and muck'

'Winter thunder, poor man's death, rich man's hunger'

'Winter never rots the sky'

'Winter's back breaks about the middle of February'

'Who doffs his coat on a winter's day, will gladly put it on in May'

'Button up to the chin till May comes in'

'If winter comes, can spring be far behind'
Shelley

'Winter time for shoeing, peascod time for wooing'

'Expect not fair weather in winter on one night's ice'

'As a winter's day lengthens, so the cold strengthens'

'He that passeth a winter's day, escapes an enemy'

And snow . . .
'Snow is the peasants' wealth'
Norwegian

'An icy May fills the granaries'
Russian

'A year of snow, a year of plenty'
  French

'Many haws, many snows'
  Scottish

'A white Christmas fills the churchyard'
  French

'Whether the weather be fine,
Whether the weather be not,
Whether the weather be cold,
Whether the weather be hot,
We'll weather the weather,
Whatever the whether,
Whether we like it or not . . .'

6

WITCHES, THE EVIL EYE AND THE DEVIL

WITCHCRAFT, VOODOO, BLACK magic and the evil eye are subjects which have fascinated man from the very earliest times. Perhaps this is because we have never been certain about their respective powers. Today we still hear of strange unexplainable happenings and the fear of the evil eye is still prevalent in many countries.

———————————— WITCHES ————————————

Most witches in medieval days tended to be women. Anyone gifted with healing power was suspected of being a witch and many were burnt. A justification for this was possibly the command given in the twenty-second chapter of Exodus namely . . . 'Thou shall not suffer a witch to live'.

It is perhaps easier and wiser to keep an open mind where the supernatural is concerned for there will always be the extra-ordinary manifestations from time to time that cannot possibly be explained.

Ambrose Bierce defined a witch as 'An ugly and repulsive old woman in a wicked league with the devil...'

or

> 'A beautiful and attractive woman in wickedness a league beyond the devil...'
> *From The Devil's Dictionary'*

'Witches and harlots come out at night'
English

'Every woman has something of a witch about her'
Spanish

'Witches cast the devil's nets'
English

'Witches and warlocks, are the devil's brood'

—————————————————— EVIL ——————————————————

'Evil shall have what evil does deserve'

'Evil enters like a needle and spreads like an oak tree'
Ethiopian

An old rhyming proverb...
> 'For every evil under the sun,
> There is a remedy or there's none,
> If there is one try to find it,
> If there's none, never mind it'

'All evils are equal when they are extreme'
English

'Sufficient unto the day is the evil thereof'
Bible

'Evil alone has oil for every wheel'

'An evil lesson is soon learned'

'There is no evil without its advantages'
Indian

'Evil report carries farther than any applause'

'Evil is sooner believed than good'

An old Malay proverb . . .
> 'The betrothed of good is evil,
> The betrothed of life is death,
> The betrothed of love is divorce'

> 'Welcome evil, if thou comest alone'

> 'In all things a man's choice is not between the good and the
> bad, but between the bad and the worse'
> *French*

THE EVIL EYE

The fear of the evil eye has always been strong in Southern and
Eastern Europe, and the old superstitions and customs linger.
Neck charms are still worn by many, coral is a well known charm
against evil, and the sewing of a red thread or cotton into the
clothes is another protection still observed. A very old idea was to
sew a small bag of salt into a coat or cloak lining thus protecting the
wearer from the evil eye whilst travelling. There are other ways to
neutralise the evil eye, to carry a piece of garlic, to have an amulet
such as a walnut, a peach stone, or simply to wear a crucifix.
Crosses made from elder wood or rowan trees are popular
amulets; old farmers used to fix these above the stable doors,
cow-pens and the dairies to protect cattle and horses.

> 'He is not called wise who knows good and ill, but he who
> can recognize of two evils the lesser'
> *Hebrew*

'Bear with evil and expect good'
French

In ancient days the Japanese would fly large kites over their homes in the shape of dragons with large staring eyes and flaring nostrils, this was to ward off the evil eye. And Chinese sailors even to this day will observe the old custom of painting an eye on the prow of a junk or small craft. If asked why, the explanation, often grudgingly given, is if a boat or ship already has an eye to see with, then it can see danger for itself and thus successfully steer the vessel to avoid it.

'Let your heart guide your head in evil matters'
Spanish

'An evil weed is soon grown'
'There are a thousand hacking at the branches of evil to one who is striking at the root'
English

'He who is bent on evil can never want lack'

'The evil that men do lives after them,
The good is oft interred with their bones'
Shakespeare

THE DEVIL

He comes in many guises: as a serpent, a goat, a sorcerer, a demon prince, a jackal, a dragon, or a gentleman even. We know him also by many different names . . . Old Nick, Lucifer, Prince of Darkness, Diabolus, Set, Beelzebub, Iblis, Mephistopheles, Old Clootie, not forgetting Old Harry, and, of course, Satan.

Everywhere, too, he has left his mark. There are countless legends and superstitions that concern him, and countless places of interest all over the world that take his name. His accredited powers, his cunning, his ability to deceive make it small wonder that there are so many references to him in both phrase and proverb, some of them so well known as to be commonplace . . .

Here are some that we all make use of daily . . .

'Needs must when the devil drives'

'The devil looks after his own'

'Between the devil and the deep blue sea'

'Better the devil you know than the devil you don't know'
'The devil take the hindmost'
'Talk of the devil and he is sure to appear'
'He who sups with the devil has need of a long spoon'
'Give the devil his due'
> *English*

'Tell the truth and shame the devil'

'The devil dances in an empty pocket'

'To hold a candle to the devil'

'The devil is not so black as he is painted'

'The devil is not always at one door'

'The devil was sick, the devil a monk would be,
The devil grew well, the devil a monk was he'

The story goes that the devil himself was an angel and he was expelled from heaven for his constant misdeeds. Since then the old legends tell us, he has vied with God to possess our souls, using his many talents and his trickery to snare the unwary. But there are those folks among us who take a more charitable view . . .

An apology for the devil . . . 'It must be remembered that we have only heard one side of the case. God has written all the books'
> *Samuel Butler*

And from Mark Twain . . .
> 'We may not pay Satan reverence, for that would be indiscreet, but we can at least respect his talents.'

A few more proverbs, some perhaps a little more unusual . . .

> 'It is an ill procession where the devil bears the cross'
> 'Where God has a temple, the devil has a chapel'
> 'Where the devil cannot come, he will send'
> *German*

> 'The devil is a busy bishop in his own diocese'
> 'The devil is not always good to beginners'
> *French*

> 'The devil places a pillow for a drunken man to fall upon'
> *Canadian*

> 'Never go to the devil and a dish-clout in your hand'
> *Scottish*

> 'The devil is seldom outshot in his own bow'
> 'Where no one will, the devil himself will bear the cross'
> *Spanish*

> 'He that takes the devil into his boat must carry him over the sound'
> *English*

> 'The devil tempts all other men, but idle men tempt the devil'
> *Turkish*

> 'The devil owed a cake and paid a loaf'
> *English*

> 'The devil never grants long leases'
> *Irish*

> 'Better keep the devil at the door than turn him out of the house'
> *Scottish*

> 'Devils live in a quiet pond'
> *Russian*

And two thought-making Yiddish proverbs . . .
'The devil comes to us in our hour of darkness, but we do not have
to let him in. And we do not have to listen either . . .'

'It was hard for Satan alone to mislead the world, so he appointed
rabbis in different localities . . .'

7
BIRDS, ANIMALS, AND INSECTS

IN MUCH EARLIER TIMES birds and animals of all kinds played a very important part in mankind's survival. Man hunted and trapped them for his food, and made use of their skins and feathers for his clothing. But as time passed he began to appreciate the different species and to take notice of their various habits and skills.

Soon birds and animals of all kinds came to be represented in cave drawings, and to decorate the walls of ancient tombs and buildings, legend and folklore and, inevitably, proverbs grew up around them . . .

──────── BIRDS ────────

'There are no birds of this year in last year's nests'

'A feather in the hand is better than a bird in the air'

'A bird in the hand is worth two in a bush'
English

'A bird can roost but on one branch, a mouse can drink not more than its fill from a river'
Chinese

'Though the bird may fly over your head, let it not make its nest in your hair'
Danish

'One beats the bush, another catches the bird?
German

'He who is not a bird should not build his nest over abysses'

'No ladder needs the bird but skies,
To situate its wings,
Nor any leader's grim baton,
Arraigns it as it sings . . .'
Emily Dickinson

CROWS

The crow was always a feared and respected bird, and still today many people regard it as a bird of ill omen . . .

'Black as night the devil's kite'
'A carrion crow never brings luck'
English

An old country saying . . .
'A crow on the thatch,
Soon death lifts the latch'

'The crow went travelling abroad and came home just as black'
English

'A crow does not louse the buffalo to clean him but to feed himself'
Hungarian

'A lonely old crow, see someone you know,
Fly to your right, sure to be right,
And if you are hawking, money before night'
Gypsy proverb

THE CUCKOO

The cuckoo is a different matter altogether, for he is the messenger of summer . . .

'In April come he will.
In May he sings all day,
In June he'll change his tune,
In July he'll fly,
In August go he must'

'Where you hear the first call of the cuckoo, there will you be

found for most of the year'
Old Hampshire proverb

'Turn your money when you hear the first cuckoo, and
you'll have money in your pocket until he comes again'
'Cuckoo song, is summer song'
English

'The cuckoo comes in April and stays the month of May,
Sings a song at Midsummer, and then goes away'

EAGLES

'The eagle does not stoop to catch flies'
'The eagle suffers little birds to sing'
Shakespeare

'The eagle never lost so much time as when he submitted to
learn of the crow'
William Blake

GEESE

Many old country people will tell you that if you have geese in the
yard you have no need of a watch-dog.

'Kill not the goose that lays the golden eggs'
English

'It is a stupid goose that listens to the fox preach'
French

'The law doth punish man or woman,
That steals the goose from off the common,
But lets the greater felon loose,
That steals the common from the goose'

'Feather by feather the goose can be plucked'
'Pluck a goose without making it scream'
French

'Sauce for the goose is sauce for the gander'
English

HENS

'Fat hens lay few eggs'
German

'You can't hatch chickens from fried eggs'
Dutch

'Better an egg today than a hen tomorrow'
French

'Never offer your hen for sale on a rainy day'
Spanish

'If a hen does not prate she'll never lay'
English

and likewise . . .
'The turtle lays thousands of eggs without anyone knowing, but when the hen lays an egg the whole country is informed'
Malay

'Pick up the hen and you can gather all the chicks'
Ashanti

'A black hen lays a white egg'
French

MAGPIES

The magpie is another bird often connected with witchcraft and death. Scottish people fear a death in the family if it flies near to the windows. Most of us however, when seeing a magpie in flight are reminded of the old magpie rhyme . . .

'One for sorrow, two for joy,
Three for a girl, four for a boy.
Five for silver, six for gold,
And seven for a secret that must never be told . . .'

OWLS

'He greatly needs a bird that gives a groat to an owl'

'The owl is the king of the night'
English

'A wise old owl lived in an oak,
The more he heard the less he spoke,
The less he spoke the more he heard,
Why can't we all be like that wise old bird?'

'I live too near a wood to be scared by owls'
Greek

PIGEONS AND PEACOCKS

'Roasted pigeons will not fly into one's mouth'
Dutch

'When the pigeons go abenting,
The farmers go lamenting'
English

'As proud as a peacock'

'Sparrows who emulate peacocks are likely to break a thigh'
Burmese

'The sparrow is sorry for the peacock at the burden of its tail'

'No peacock envies another peacock his tail'
Latin

RAVENS

'He that takes the raven for his guide will light on carrion'

'Raise ravens and they will peck out your eyes'
Spanish

The well-known ravens at the Tower of London are cherished birds. The old superstition is that should the birds die out or, worse still, leave the Tower, then the reigning royal house would fall and the country with it.

ROBINS

Robins have always been largely figured in fable and folklore, there are many old legends and tales told of them, the most popular perhaps is the crucifixion legend. Not only did the robin accompany Christ on his weary journey to Calvary, it also tried to pick the thorns from his brow, thus staining its breast red, hence the name 'robin redbreast'

'He that hurts a robin will never prosper'
Cornish

And from Devon comes this old saying . . .
'If you touch a robin's nest, you will have a crooked finger all your life . . .'

SWALLOWS

'One swallow does not make a summer'

'One swallow makes not a spring, nor a woodcock a winter'

Thrushes . . .
'That's the wise thrush; he sings his song twice over,
Lest you should think he never could recapture,
The first fine careless rapture'
Robert Browning

'Wild ducks and tomorrow both come without calling'
Russian

Now fourfooted friends cloven and otherwise . . .

ASSES .

'Every ass loves to hear himself bray'

'No wise man stands behind an ass when he kicks'

'Hay is more acceptable to an ass than gold'
Latin

'The ass that is common property is always the worst saddled'
English

'The ass loaded with gold still eats thistles'
German

'An ass may bray a good while before he shakes the stars down'
George Eliot

'I had rather ride on an ass that carries me than a horse that throws me'
George Herbert

'Even if an ass goes travelling he'll not come home a horse'
English

CATS

Centuries ago cats were sacred in many eastern countries. Some races believed that when a person died his spirit would enter the body of a cat. The ancient Chinese worshipped cats because of their ability to see in the dark which meant that they could easily detect the fearful demons who haunted the night. They painted pictures of cats on their houses for further protection and believed, in common with the early Greeks, that the waxing and waning of the moon was reflected in the widening and narrowing of a cat's pupils.

The cat-headed goddess Bast used to be the symbol of fertility and happiness, she was worshipped by the Egyptians nearly 3,000 years ago. They wore bracelets and amulets with a cat motif engraved upon them, and decorated their homes with weird drawings and paintings of cats.

'A cat has nine lives'

'Cats in mittens catch no mice'

'While the cat's away, the mice can play'

'Curiosity killed the cat'

'That which comes of a cat will catch mice'
English

'A cat may look at a king'

'A cat pent up becomes a lion'
Italian

'Wanton kittens make sober cats'
English

'The cats that drive the mice away are as good as they that catch them'
German

'Well knows the cat whose ear she licks'
'Cats like man are flatterers'
French

'Like a cat on hot bricks'
English

'I am the cat of cats. I am
the everlasting cat!
Cunning and old and sleek as jam,
The everlasting cat!
I hunt the vermin in the night,
The everlasting cat,
For I see best without the light,
The everlasting cat.'
William Brighty Rands

COWS

'Better kiss your cow than your enemy'

'Milk the cow that standeth still'

'Many a good cow hath a bad calf'

'As nimble as a cow in a cage'
English

'Bring a cow into the hall and she'll run the byre'
Scottish

'Cow of many, well milked and badly fed'
Spanish

'He that owns the cow goes nearest the tail'

'A curst cow has short horns'

DOGS

Dogs, said to be the ever faithful friend of man . . .

'A dog will never forget the crumb thou gavest him, though thou
mayst afterwards throw a hundred stones at his head'
James Ross

'Don't keep a dog and bark yourself'
'Every dog hath its day'
English

And of barking dogs . . .

'The old dog barks not in vain'
French

'Dogs that bark at a distance never bite'
English

'A dog does not always bark at the front gate'
Spanish

'When one dog barks another will join it'
Latin

'The slowest barker is the surest biter'
French

'When the old dog barks it is time to watch'
Latin

'Let dogs delight to bark and bite,
For God hath made them so,
Let bears and lions growl and fight,
For 'tis their nature too'
Isaac Watts

'A dog will not howl if you beat him with a bone'

'He that hath nothing to spare must not keep a dog'

'Beware of a silent dog and still water'
German

'The hindmost dog may catch the hare'

'Who gives bread to other's dogs is often barked at by
his own'
Italian

'Give a dog a bad name and it will hang him'

'Let sleeping dogs lie'
'Dog does not eat dog'
English

'Modest dogs miss much meat'

THE FOX

Country folk through the ages have all learned to be wary of the fox, His clever, cunning ways they have grudgingly admired, his skill and his craft have earned him a special place in folk-lore and legend. Even today there is still much controversy about hunting and killing the fox. Once foxes' tongues were worn as amulets against evil, a farmer might nail a fox brush above the door of his stable or cowbyre to protect his livestock from the evil eye.

'The fox knows much, but more he that catcheth him'

'The tail doth often catch the fox'

'With foxes we must play the fox'

'The fox condemns the trap, not himself'
William Blake

'An old fox understands the trap'

'Old foxes want no tutors'

'He that will get the better of a fox must rise early'
French

'When the fox preaches, beware the geese'
English

'An old fox need learn no craft'

'Foxes dig not their own holes'

'The fox may grow grey but never good'

'The wiles of the fox will never enter the lion's head'

'Every fox must pay his own skin to the flayer'

And from the old Dene Indians of Arctic Canada comes this quaint riddle...
'What comes down the mountain flashing like fire?'
— A red fox's tail

'A foolish fox is caught by one leg, but a wise one by all four.'
Serbian proverb

'A wise fox will never rob his neighbours henroost'
French

HORSES

The horse was a sacred animal to early man and was always connected with much old fable and legend. These patient creatures have carried men to battle, ploughed faithfully many an acre, and were always steadfastly protected from witchcraft and the evil eye throughout the centuries. Horse-brasses were designed in the shape of suns with projecting rays, or crescent moons, wheat-sheaves and many other amulets. In some countries the horse was regarded as a symbol of fertility, far surpassing any other animal. Indian warriors thought more of their horses than their women-folk and children, not unlike that stolid race of ploughmen, carters, grooms, blacksmiths and stableboys.
Naturally, proverbs abound concerning this noble animal...

'Who has a good horse in his stable can go afoot'

'Have a horse of thine own and thou mayst borrow another's'
Welsh

'The man who does not love a horse cannot love a woman'
Spanish

'If two men ride a horse, one must ride behind'

Three similar ones . . .
>'One may ride a free horse to death'
>>*Scottish*
>'A hired horse a tired horse never'
>'A pair of spurs to a borrowed horse is better than a peck of oats'
>>*Yorkshire*

>'The stable wears out a horse more than the road'
>>*French*

>'One cannot shoe a running horse'
>>*Dutch*

>'The old horse may die waiting for the new grass'
>>*Chinese*

>'The old horse must die in someone's keeping'

>'A man may lead a horse to water, but cannot make him drink'
>>*English*

>'Let a horse drink when he will, not what he will'

A proverbial rhyme from Berkshire . . .
>'Up-hill spare me,
>Down-hill forbear me,
>Plain way spare me not,
>Let me not drink when I am hot'

Gipsies have a way with horses, here are some typical gipsy proverbs . . .

>'Good horses can't be of a bad colour'

>'A dapple-grey horse will sooner die than tire'

>'Flies go to lean horses'

>'In selling a horse praise his bad points, and leave the good ones to look after themselves'

>'The buyer needs a hundred eyes, the horse thief not one'

>'If you meet a piebald horse, wish before you see his tail'
>>*New Forest gipsies*

'Trust not a horse's heel nor a dog's tooth'

'One white foot buy him,
Two white feet try him,
Three white feet look well about him,
Four white feet leave him alone'

To follow the gipsy rhyme one or two more old gipsy proverbs . . .

'A cough will stick longer by a horse than a peck of oats'

'Water trotted is as good as oats'

'He that hath a white horse and a fair wife need never want for trouble'

'One man may better steal a horse than another look on'

'A shoemaker made shoes without leather,
Of all the elements taken together,
Earth, water, fire and air,
And every customer had two pair'
— A Horseshoe
Old rhyming riddle

More horsey proverbs, many we use every day so commonplace are they . . .

'Don't look a gift horse in the mouth'

'All lay load on the willing horse'

'Don't judge a horse by the harness'

'Nothing so bold as a blind mare'

'One saddle is enough for one horse'

'A horseshoe that clatters wants a nail'
Spanish

And this proverb brings at once to mind the old nursery rhyme...
'For the want of a nail, the shoe was lost,
For the want of a shoe, the horse was lost,
For want of a horse, the rider was lost,
For want of a rider the battle was lost,
For the want of a battle the kingdom was lost,
And all for the want of a horseshoe nail'

SHEEP & LAMBS

Much old shepherd's lore is evident in these proverbs concerning lambs and sheep...

'There is a black sheep in every flock'

'One foolish sheep will lead the flock'

'It is a foolish sheep that makes a wolf its confessor'

'He that has one sheep in the flock will like all the rest the better for it'
Scottish

'A pet lamb makes a cross ram'

'May as well be hanged for a sheep as a lamb'
English

'A bad shearer never had a good sickle'
French

'Shear your sheep when elder blossoms peep'

'The wool seller knows the wool buyer'
Yiddish

'Many go out for wool and come home shorn'

'You were better given the wool than the sheep'

It is an old superstition among country folk that during lambing time every shepherd will look eagerly for a jet black lamb in his flock. Such a lamb will be the mascot of the flock, the luck bringer.

MICE

'In baiting a mousetrap with cheese, always leave room for the mouse'
Greek

'It is a bold mouse that nestles in the cat's ear'
English

'Not the mouse is the thief, but the hole in the wall'
Yiddish

'When the mouse laughs at the cat there is a hole nearby'
Nigerian

'A mouse in time may bite a cable in two'

'Burn not your house to fright away the mice'
Thomas Fuller

'Better a mouse in the pot than no flesh at all'
Italian

LIONS, LEOPARDS & TIGERS

'If the lion's skin will not do, we must sew on that of the fox'
Latin

'Even a hare will insult a dead lion'
Latin

'You can tell the lion by his paw'

'Lions in peace, deer in war'

'He that has gone so far as to cut the claws of a lion, will not feel himself secure until he has drawn his teeth'
Charles Caleb Colton

'Can the Ethiopian change his skin, or the leopard his spots'
Bible

'Rain beats a leopard's skin, but it does not wash off
the spots'
Ashanti

'Unless you enter the tiger's den you cannot take the cubs'
Japanese

'He who rides the tiger can never dismount'
Chinese

'Those who hunt deer sometimes raise tigers'
Indian

And a very thought-provoking proverb from China . . .
'Before dinner, let us explore the southern plains and climb
the northern mountains. After dinner, there are snakes in
the southern plains and tigers in the northern mountains'

'Tiger, tiger burning bright,
In the forests of the night,
What immortal hand or eye,
Could frame thy fearful symmetry'
William Blake

PIGS

'Pigs might fly, but they are most unlikely birds'

'Pigs grow fat where lambs would starve'

'A hog on trust grunts till he's paid'

'A pretty pig makes an ugly sow'

'To buy a pig in a poke'

'A pig that has two owners is sure to die of hunger'

'Casting pearls before swine'

BEARS

'He must have iron nails that would scratch a bear'

'The old bear falls into the old trap'
    Russian

'As cross as a bear with a sore head'
    English

'Little bears have all their troubles to come'

RABBITS AND HARES

'If three dogs chase a rabbit they cannot kill it'
    English

'As mad as a March hare'

'To run with the hare and hunt with the hounds'

'Hares can gambol over the body of a dead lion'

THE OX

'An old ox ploughs a straight furrow'

'Take heed of an ox before, as an ass behind, and a monk on all sides'
Spanish

'When the ox stumbles, all whet their knives'
Yiddish

'An ox with long horns, even if he does not butt, will be accused of butting'
Malay

'The stolen ox sometimes puts his head out of the stall'
Spanish

'An ox remains an ox, even if driven to Vienna'
Hungarian

'One hair of a woman draws more than a team of oxen'
English

'An old ox will find shelter for himself'

'A man must plough with such oxen as he hath'

RATS

The ancient Egyptians had a great respect for rats, firstly because they were the symbol of utter destruction, and secondly because they were always wise in their judgements. A rat would always choose the best bread to gnaw, find the best grain, and sense coming disaster. They would also desert a doomed ship, and leave a house or barn scheduled for burning or destruction.

Unusual charms were kept to protect stored grain from rats in earlier days. A hot cross bun from Good Friday's baking might be hung in the granary, stranger still, the following method was used if the rats were extremely troublesome. A letter would be written with words to the effect that the farmer or owner of the barn recommended a change of dwelling for the rat colony. Directions were carefully given guiding the rats to another farm where they would be safer and snugger during the winter months. The small

piece of paper was then well greased with goose grease and pushed
well down into one of the rat holes. And old farmers insisted that
this method was foolproof, within a day or so the rats would be
gone.

'An old rat is a brave rat'
'To a good rat, a good cat'
'Rats desert a sinking ship'
'To take the rat by the tail'
French

THE WOLF

'Men must have corrupted nature a little, for they were not
born wolves, and they have become wolves'
Voltaire

'Man is a wolf to man'
Latin

Similarly . . .

'Man is not man, but a wolf to those he does not know'
French

'The wolf loses his teeth, but not his inclinations'
Spanish

'To cry wolf'

'No matter how much you feed a wolf he will always
return to the forest'
Russian

'The wolf knows what the ill beast thinks'
French

'The wolf changes his coat but not his nature'
Latin

ANTS & BEES

Numerous insects too have been mentioned in proverbs . . .

'An ant hole may collapse an embankment'
Japanese

'Where does the ant die except in sugar'
Malay

'In the ants' house the dew is a flood'
Persian

'Ants and savages put strangers to death'
Bertrand Russell

There are many curious tales and superstitions told about bees,
for instance, 'telling the bees' when a member of the family dies.
If this should be omitted, then it is quite possible that the bees may
desert their hive. This seems reasonable enough, bees in common
with animals get used to their owner's voice, and probably dislike
change. And another old country superstition, money must not
be exchanged for bees as the old rhyme tells us . . .

'If you wish your bees to thrive,
Gold must be paid with every hive,
For when they're bought with other money,
There will be neither swarm nor honey'

'Swine, woman, and bees, cannot be turned'

'The earth is a beehive, we all enter by the same door'
African

'The best honey isn't got by squeezing'

'Every bee's honey is sweet'
'What is not good for the swarm is not good for the bees'
French

'While honey lies in every flower no doubt,
It takes a bee to get the honey out'
Arthur Guiterman

FLIES & FLEAS

'Every beetle is a gazelle in the eyes of its mother'

'When they came to shoe the horses, the beetle stretched
out his leg'

Someone said once . . . 'The fly ought to be used as the symbol of impertinence and audacity, for whilst all other animals shun man more than anything else, and run away before he comes near them, the fly lights right upon his very nose!'

'Don't imitate the fly before you have wings'
French

'A fly may sting a horse and make him wince'
English

'The flea though he kill none, he does all the harm he can'
John Donne

'Great fleas have little fleas upon their backs to bite 'em'
And little fleas have lesser fleas, and so on *ad infinitum*'

'The parasites live where the great have little secret sores'

'Do nothing hastily but the catching of fleas'
Thomas Fuller

'Who lies with dogs shall rise up with fleas'
Latin

'A reasonable amount of fleas is good for dog, it keeps him from brooding'

SPIDERS

'If you wish to live and thrive, let a spider run alive'

'A spider in the morning sorrow brings,
At evening dusk, good luck he brings'

'When spider webs unite, they can tie up a lion'
Ethiopian

'The spider as an artist, has never been employed,
Though his surpassing merit, is freely certified'
Emily Dickinson

This old rhyme includes both animal, bird and insect and seems a fitting way to end this chapter . . .

'The dog will come when he is called,
The cat will walk away,

The monkey's cheek is very bald,
The goat is fond of play.
The pig is not a feeder nice,
The squirrel loves a nut,
The wolf would eat you in a trice,
The buzzard's eyes are shut,
The lark sings high in the air,
The linnet in the tree,
The swan he has a bosom fair,
And who so proud as he?
The little wren is very small,
The humming bird is less,
The ladybird is least of all,
And beautiful in dress . . .'

8

FROM THE CRADLE TO THE GRAVE

CHILDHOOD

'Blessed be childhood, which brings down something of heaven into the midst of our rough earthliness'
Henri Frederic Amiel

Long remembered are those things that we learnt in our childhood; old rhymes, sayings, superstitions and proverbs they remain with us for most of our days . . .

'Monday's child is fair of face,
Tuesday's child is full of grace,
Wednesday's child is full of woe,
Thursday's child has far to go;
Friday's child is loving and forgiving,
Saturday's child works hard for a living,
But the child that is born on the Sabbath day,
Is merry and happy, and bright and gay . . .'

And how many times have we heard this old proverb? and perhaps the others that follow it... 'Children should be seen and not heard'

'Little pitchers have big ears'

'What the children hear at home soon flies abroad'

'The child says nothing but what it heard by the fire'

'What a mother sings to the cradle goes all the way to the coffin'
Henry Beecher Ward

From Robert Louis Stevenson...
'A child should always say what's true,
And speak when he is spoken to,
And behave mannerly at table,
At least so far as he is able...'

'Who takes the child by the hand takes the mother by the heart'
Danish

'Children pick up words as pigeons peas,
And utter them again as God shall please'
Old English proverb

PARENTS

'Govern a small family as you would cook a small fish, very gently'
Chinese

'Give a little love to a child, and you get a great deal back'
John Ruskin

'Children are poor men's riches'
English

'Children are the anchors that hold a mother to life'
Sophocles

'The child may be rocked too hard'
French

'A child may have too much of his mother's blessing'
Scottish

'A rich child often sits in a poor mother's lap'
Danish

'The child who gets a stepmother also gets a stepfather'
Greek

YOUTH

'Youth has a small head'
Irish

'Young folk silly folk, old folk cold folk'
Dutch

'Young men think old men are fools, but old men know young men are fools'

'Youth looks forward but age looks back'
English

or . . .

'Young men look forward,
Old men look backward,
The middle-aged look around . . .'

'Youth will be served'
English

'Young wood makes a hot fire'
Greek

'Raw leather will soon stretch'

'He that spares when he is young may spend when he is old'

111

'Stretch your foot to the length of your blanket'
   Persian

'Man is like palm wine; when young sweet, but without strength, but in age, strong and harsh'
   Congolese

'Youth is perpetual intoxication; it is a fever of the mind'
   La Rochefoucauld

'Our youth we can have but today,
We may always find time to grow old'

'A young branch takes on all the bends that one gives it'
   Chinese

'Alas that Spring should vanish with the rose,
That youth's sweet manuscript should close . . .'
   Omar Khayyam

'Young men forgive, old men never'
   French

'Growth is the only evidence of life'

'No man is quick enough to enjoy life to the full'
   Spanish

'Young people don't know what age is, and old people forget what youth was'

'Be jogging while your boots are still green'
   Irish

'Learn young, learn fair; learn old, learn more'
Scottish

'A wild colt may become a sober horse'

'At twenty the will rules,
At thirty the intellect,
At forty the judgement'
Baltasar Gracian

—————— LOVE AND LOVERS ——————

It was Francis Bacon who said . . . 'It is impossible to love and be wise' . . . and Confucius who said . . . 'To love a thing means wanting it to live . . .'

Since it seems that we may all of us fall in and out of love at any age, here is a selection of proverbs that deal with that elusive emotion . . .

'A lover without indiscretion is no lover at all'
Thomas Hardy

'Love enters a man through his eyes, woman through her ears'
Polish

and . . .

'Though love be blind, yet 'tis not for want of eyes'

'The eyes are always children'
French

'A man has choice to begin love, but not end it'

'Fair is not fair but that which pleaseth'

'Nobody's sweetheart is ugly'
Dutch

'Love can be a violent emotion for some'
French

'The more violent the love, the more violent the anger'
Burmese

'Love is a tyrant sparing none'

'Try to reason about love and you will lose your reason'
    French

'Love is like war; begin when you like and leave off when
you can'
    Spanish

Warnings for lovers . . .
    'Never love with all your heart, it only ends in breaking'
    'They love too much that die for love'
        English

And from Samuel Johnson . . . 'Love is the wisdom of the fool
and the folly of the wise'

'No folly like being in love'
    Latin

'Where there is love there is pain'
    Spanish

'The pleasure of love lasts but a moment,
The pain of love lasts a lifetime'
    French

'A mighty pain to love it is,
And it is a pain that pain to miss;
But of all pains the greatest pain,
It is to love, but love in vain . . .
    Abraham Cowley

'True love never runs smoothly'

'The lover loves not at all that knows when to make an end'

'They who love most are least valued'
   English

'As the best wine makes the sharpest vinegar, the truest
lover may turn into the worst enemy'

'Where love fails we espy all faults'
   English

'A broken hand works, but not a broken heart'
   Persian

'Love is like the measles; we all have to go through it.
Also like the measles we only really take it once...'
   Jerome K. Jerome

'Love is an excuse for its own faults'
   Italian

'The greatest love is a mother's;
Then comes a dog's,
Then comes a sweetheart's...'
   Polish

A wise Yiddish proverb... 'Love is sweet, but tastes best with
bread'

MARRIAGE

Hints for husbands... and those about to marry...

'Marriage is a covered dish'

'Choose neither a woman nor linen by candlelight'
   Italian

'One should choose one's bedfellow whilst it is daylight'
   Swedish

'Pray one hour before going to war,
Two hours before going to sea,
And three hours before getting married'
   Old Indian proverb

'Lips however rosy must be fed'

'Marriage is a lottery'
> *French*

'Age and wedlock bring a man to his nightcap'

'A wooer should open his ears more than his eyes'
> *Norwegian*

'Choose a wife on a Saturday rather than a Sunday'
likewise
> 'Sunday's wooing draws to ruin'

'If you want a fine wife, don't pick her on a Sunday'
> *Spanish*

And if you marry for money . . .

'He that marries for wealth sells his liberty'
> *English*

'He that marries for money will earn it'
> *American*

'Where there is dowry there is danger'
> *Irish*

'Better a fortune in a wife than with a wife'

'Silk and velvet put out the kitchen fire'
> *German*

'Who marrieth for love without money hath good nights and sorry days'

Hints for wives . . .
> 'Marriage is the supreme blunder that all women make'

'The most fascinating women never make the best marriages'

'The clever wife makes her husband an apron'
> *French*

'Discreet wives have neither eyes nor ears'
> *English*

'Every woman should marry, but no man'
> *Benjamin Disraeli*

'There is no perfect marriage, for there are no perfect men'
French

'An old maid who marries becomes a young wife'
'Parents can give a dowry, but not good luck'
Yiddish

'Wives are young men's mistresses, companions for the middle age, and old men's nurses'
Francis Bacon

Widows...
Some rather cynical proverbs about widows from various countries...

'Never marry a widow unless her first husband was hanged'
'He that marries a widow will often have a dead man's head thrown into the dish'
Spanish

'He that marries a widow with four children marries four thieves'
Italian

'Never marry a widow, because she has cast her rider'

'Long a widow weds with shame'
English

'Sorrow for a widow is like pain in the elbow, sharp and short'
French

'Marry a widow before she leave mourning'

'The rich widow cries with one eye and laughs with the other'

MOTHERS-IN-LAW

And, inevitably, mothers-in-law ... both partners in a marriage gain a mother-in-law, and these unfortunate ladies seem to bear the brunt of the sharpest of marital proverbs and sayings. Old Indian warriors in one tribe, who shall be nameless, solved their particular mother-in-law problems in this way. They first chose their intended wife and then proceeded to court her mother. By marrying first the mother and then the daughter, they could then be quite certain of no interfering mother-in-law!

'There is but one good mother-in-law and she is dead'
English

'The best mother-in-law wears a green overcoat'
New Forest

'There is no good mother-in-law but that she wears a green gown'
French

'A mother-in-law is what you inherit when you marry'
English

'Mothers-in-law arrive on the twelve o'clock broom'

'A son is a son till he gets him a wife,
But a daughter's a daughter the rest of your life'

'No mother-in-law ever remembers that she was once a daughter-in-law'

'A mother-in-law's coming is another mouth to heed'

'She is the happiest wife that marries the son of a dead mother'

'A mother takes some twenty years to mould her son in her own image; just to see some other woman make a fool of him in as many minutes . . .'

OLD AGE

This unfortunately creeps up on us all relentlessly and folds us around like a cloak. Happily many of us can wear it cheerfully and well, and even grow to accept it, those that can't still have to wear it and accept it anyway . . .

'A man is as old as he feels himself to be'
English

'A man as he manages himself, may die old at thirty, or young at eighty'

'Dying young is a boon in old age'
Yiddish

'The tragedy of old age is not that one is old, but that one is young'
Oscar Wilde

'Age does not give sense it only makes one go slowly'
Finnish

'The real dread of man is not the devil, but old age'
'Age can be a bad travelling companion'
English

'Old age is not total misery, experience helps'
Euripides

'Only he that has travelled the road knows where the holes are deep'
Chinese

'Few people know how to be old'
La Rochefoucauld

'No one is so old that he does not think he could live another year'

'With the ancient is wisdom; and in the length of days understanding'
Bible

'I love everything that's old;
old friends, old times, old manners,
old books, old wines . . .'
Oliver Goldsmith

'But old age can have its pleasures, which, though different are not less than the pleasures of youth . . .' — comforting words from W. Somerset Maugham. Here are one or two more proverbs in the same vein . . .

'An old man loved is winter with flowers'
German

'Growing old is no more than another bad habit'
Spanish

'As we grow old, beauty steals inward'
Emerson

'There are toys for all ages'
French

'Old age is venerable'
Latin

'Age is opportunity no less,
Than youth itself, though in another dress,
And as the evening twilight fades away,
The sky is filled with stars, invisible by day . . .'
Longfellow

DEATH

There are many traditions and customs concerned with death, backed up with proverbs, sayings and superstitions. Not many are heeded now, and the dead depart this life in a very well-ordered way with the briefest of ceremonies. Funeral feasts are past, as are the hired mourners who wore their sprig of rosemary in the buttonhole, which was later dropped into the grave. Old courtesy demanded that cakes, wines and spirits were offered before the coffin was 'lifted'. After the lifting all the family and mourners took their leave of the corpse, and followed it respectfully to the graveyard.

Black was worn, and in the case of titled families with many servants as mourners, black hatbands, armbands, and gloves would be duly handed out for the sad occasion.

'Death is the grand leveller'
Thomas Fuller

'Death is a camel that lies down at every door'
Persian

'Death pays all debts'
English

'Flowers and buds fall, and the old and ripe fall'
Malay

'Death does not blow a trumpet'

'Few are wholly dead,
Blow on a dead man's embers,
And a live flame will start'
    Robert Graves

'Death always comes too early or too late'
    English

'Death cancels everything but truth'

'To die completely, a person must not only forget, but be
forgotten, and he who is not forgotten is not dead'
    Samuel Butler

'Our last garment is made without pockets'
    Italian

'A man can only die once'
    English

'Death closes all doors'
    English

'The coffin is the brother of the cradle'
    German

'Even a coffin is made to measure'
    Russian

'Nothing seems worse to a man than his death, and yet it
may be the height of his good luck'
    Irish

'Deaths foreseen come not'

'We never know we go when we are going,
We jest and shut the door,
Fate, following behind us bolts it,
And we accost no more . . .'
    Emily Dickinson

'Young men may die, old men must'
    English

'Death devours lambs as well as sheep'
'Do not make an enemy of death'

9

THE WISDOM OF
THE SEASONS

---------------------- TIME ----------------------

NOTHING EVADES US SO utterly as time, it slips away as silently as a thief. The seasons come and go all too soon . . .

'Who is not ready today, will not be ready tomorrow'

'Time is a file that wears and makes no noise'
   English

'Time is, time was, time is past'

'What may be done at anytime will be done at no time'

'There is a time for all things'
   English

'A stone thrown at the right time is better than gold given at the wrong time'
   Persian

'Time deals gently only with those who take it gently'
   Anatole France

'Time flies over us, but leaves its shadow behind'
   Nathaniel Hawthorne

'Time flies you say?
No, no,
Time stays,
You go!'

'As good have no time as make no good use of it'
'No time like the present'
'Time and thinking tame the strongest grief'
   English

'Procrastination is the thief of time'

'Time brings all things to pass'

'Years following years steal something every day,
At last they steal us from ourselves away . . .'
  Alexander Pope

'Take old Time by the forelock'

'Accusing the times is but excusing ourselves'
  Thomas Fuller

'In time take time, when time does last,
For time is no time when time is past'

THE SEASONS

'To every thing there is a season, and a time to every
purpose under heaven'
  Bible

'Every season brings its own joy'
  Spanish

'Sing a song of seasons,
Something bright in all,
Flowers in the summer,
Fires in the fall . . .'
  Robert Louis Stevenson

SPRING

'Don't say that spring has come until you can put your foot
on nine daisies'
  Old Hampshire proverb

'A late spring is a great blessing'
  English

'A January spring is worth nothing'

'In the spring a young man's fancy lightly turns to thoughts
of love'
  Alfred, Lord Tennyson

Spring is Nature's birth time, a time of new beginnings, thought by many to be the loveliest time of the year. Blossom comes to the trees, lambs race in the fields, and the birds are busy nesting, everywhere there is evidence of new life. Primroses and daffodils are in our gardens, country children still seek the first cowslips and the farmer is busy with the ploughing. The ancient proverb comes to mind . . . 'Spring arrives on the heel of winter'

'Spring brings health, heralding summer's wealth'
  Norwegian

'Each thing is fair when it is young'
  Estonian

'The first dish pleaseth all'
  Scottish

'In spring no one thinks of the snow that fell last year'
  Swedish

SUMMER

'The sun shines upon all alike'
  English

'The sun does not shine on both sides of the hedge at once'

'He who bathes in May,
Will soon be laid in clay;
He who bathes in June
Will sing a merry tune;
He who bathes in July,
Must dance till he is dry'

'A summer's sun is worth the having'
  French

A rather quaint old riddle from Israel . . .
> 'Every one loves me so,
> Nobody can bear to see me go . . .
> What am I?
> — The summer

And at the end of summer comes the harvest, one of the busiest times for farming folk everywhere. The fragrant hay harvest begins towards the end of June, and the grain harvest sometime in August. The harvest-home was once a great feast taking much preparation, often called the most important feast of the rural year, apart from Christmas of course. The horses that drew the harvest carts wore red ribbons to keep witches and warlocks at bay, and the traditional corn dolly was made from the last of the sheaves and borne in triumphantly to sit at the head of the huge harvest table.

> 'We have ploughed, we have sowed,
> We have reaped, we have mowed,
> We have brought home every load,
> Hip! Hip! Hip! Harvest home! . . .'

'Two good haymakers are worth twenty boasters'

'Even after a bad harvest there must be sowing'
> *Latin*

'Better reap two days too soon than one day too late'
> *English*

'Cutting out well is better than sewing up well'
> *Scottish*

'Provide in leisure to use in haste'

'Once in motion, to push a cart is easy'

'A good reaper does not neglect his scythe'

Another Harvest rhyme . . .
> 'Let the wealthy and great,
> Roll in splendour and state,
> I envy them not I declare it.
> I eat my own lamb, my own chicken and ham,
> I sheer my own fleece, and I wear it.

I have fruit, I have flowers,
I have lawns, I have bowers,
The lark is my morning alarming.
So jolly boys now,
Here's God-speed to the plough,
Long life and success to all farming . . .'

AUTUMN

'Autumn steals summer like a thief'
English

Inevitably the leaves fall in the autumn. Country folk in many parts of the world share the old belief that if the leaves wither on the boughs instead of falling to the ground in the usual way, then this tells of a very cold winter to follow. Also, if the weather is mild at the end of October the winter might well be wet, or, if cold, sometimes one hears this old rhyme quoted . . .

'If ducks do slide at Hallowtide,
At Christmas they will swim;
If ducks do swim at Hallowtide,
At Christmas they will slide . . .'

'Autumn is the hush before winter'
French

An ancient superstition . . .
'Every falling leaf which can be caught in the hand in autumn, means a happy month the following year'

All Hallows, the last night of October, was often regarded in much earlier days as the most haunted night of the year. It was the night when witches, demons, ghosts, and all manner of evil spirits came back to earth to wander at will, and in general to create as much havoc as possible. Farmers locked their cattle away safely, nobody went out on this night if they could possibly avoid it.

French people would put apples and nuts in a small bowl near to the hearth; it was widely believed that witches and evil spirits were afraid of these fruits. The early settlers from England took many of these old superstitions with them, so that where they made their homes, in parts of Canada, and America, the old Hallow'en customs and superstitions were kept up . . .

'All Hallows moon, witches soon'
Canada

'A fair October and a good blast, will blow the hag and her broom away fast . . .'
Old English

——— WINTER ———

The coming of Christmas puts a sparkle into the dark days of December . . .

'If Christmas day be fine and clear, corn and hay will then be dear'

'Light Christmas, light wheatsheaf; dark Christmas, heavy wheatsheaf'
English

'If Christmas ice hangs on the willow, clover may be cut at Easter'

'Christmas is coming, the goose is getting fat,
Please spare a penny for the old man's hat;
If you haven't got a penny, a ha'penny will do,
If you haven't got a ha'penny, God bless you . . .'

An old country proverb . . .
'If Christmas Day on Thursday be, a windy winter ye shall see;
windy weather in each week, and hard tempest strong and thick.
The summer shall be good and dry, corn and beasts shall multiply'

THE NEW YEAR

'The New Year is a new beginning'
English

'The year does nothing else but open or shut'
Danish

A riddle of the year from Norway . . .

'A tree stands on Reine;
It has twelve golden boughs,
Four nests on each bough
And seven eggs in each nest,
And the seventh is of gold'

(This, of course, refers to the year, the months, weeks and days,
including Sunday.)

'Ring out the old, ring in the new,
Ring, happy bells, across the snow,
The year is going, let him go,
Ring out the false, ring in the new . . .'
Alfred, Lord Tennyson

THE DAYS OF THE YEAR

'Yesterday, to-day, and to-morrow, are the three days of man'

'Come day, go day, and God send Sunday'

'Thursday come, and the week is gone'

'Yesterday will not be called again'

'Day by day passes until the last stands behind the door'
  Burmese

'Every day learns from the one that went before, but no day teaches the one that follows'
  Russian

'Each day provides its own gifts'
  American

'Praise not the day before night'
  Thomas Fuller

'Every day cannot be a feast of lanterns'
  Chinese

'The next day is never so good as the day before'

'Sufficient unto the day is the evil thereof'
  Bible

'Come what come may,
Time and the hour,
Runs through the roughest day'
  William Shakespeare

'What a day may bring, a day may take away'
  Thomas Fuller

'The day is done, and the darkness,
Falls from the wings of night,
As a feather is wafted downward,
From an eagle in his flight . . .'
  Longfellow

TOMORROW

'Tomorrow never comes'

'Tomorrow is often the busiest day of the week'
  Spanish

'Never put off till tomorrow what may be done today'
'Tomorrow is a new day'
'One today, is worth two tomorrows'
  English

'Tomorrow your horse may be lame'
  Yiddish

'Often do the spirits,
Of great events stride on before the events,
And in today, already walks tomorrow'
  Samuel Taylor Coleridge

'We steal if we touch tomorrow. It is God's'
  Henry Beecher Ward

'They who lose today may win tomorrow'

'Defer not till tomorrow to be wise,
Tomorrow's sun to thee may never rise'
  William Congreve

'One of these days is none of these days'
  English

'Today it may be a fire, tomorrow it will be ashes'
  Arabic

'When God says today, the devil says tomorrow'
  German

'Life is made up of tomorrows'
  French

'Business today, tomorrow never'
  Spanish

'Happy the man, and happy he alone,
He who can call today his own,

He who, secure within, can say,
Tomorrow, do thy worst, for I
have lived today ...'
    John Dryden

'People live for the tomorrow, because the day-after-tomorrow is doubtful'

YESTERDAY

'Today is yesterday's pupil'

'When you get to the top, don't look back'
    Yiddish

'We are but of yesterday, and know nothing, because our days on earth are a shadow'
    Bible

'Yesterday's promise, like tomorrow's never comes'
    German

'Yesterday is not easy to recover, but tomorrow we can win or lose'

'Time and words can't be recalled, even if it was only yesterday'
    Yiddish

'Yesterday is nostalgia'
    French

'We are not free to use today, or to promise tomorrow, because we are already mortgaged to yesterday ...'
    Emerson

131

10
PROVERBS FROM MANY LANDS

---------------------- CHINESE ----------------------

Confucius, that wise and learned philosopher, has been credited with hundreds of meaningful sayings and proverbs; whether he was actually responsible for even a half of them would be difficult to establish. Some of his proverbs are included in the following:

'He who heard the truth in the morning might die content in the evening'

'He who has really set his mind on virtue will do no evil'
    Confucius

'I was angered, for I had no shoes. Then I met a man who had no feet'

'A needle is not sharp at both ends'

'A murder may be forgiven, an affront never'

'Blessings do not come in pairs; misfortunes never come singly'

Misfortune is not that which can be avoided, but that which cannot'

'There is no one to sweep a common hall'

'A diamond with a flaw is worth more than a pebble without imperfections'

'Prepare for calamity not yet in bud'

'It is not the knowing that is difficult, but the doing'

'The wise adapt themselves to circumstances, as water moulds itself to the pitcher'

'Virtue never dwells alone; it always has neighbours'

'He who governs by his moral excellence may be compared to the Pole star which abides in its place while all other stars bow towards it'

'Artful speech and an ingratiating demeanour rarely accompany virtue'
Confucius

'The Gods cannot help those who do not seize opportunities'

Three rather cynical sayings, nevertheless amusing . . .

'One man will carry two buckets of water for his own use,
Two men will carry one for their joint use;
Three men will carry none for anybody's use'

'Do not remove a fly from your friend's forehead with a hatchet'

'When the butcher dies, do you think we shall eat our pork with the bristles on?'

'Men trip not on mountains; they trip on molehills'

'The one legged never stumble'

'When you bow, bow low'

'Small men think they are small; great men never know they are great'

'A man without a smiling face must not open shop'

'To open a shop is easy, to keep it open is an art'

'A dog in a kennel barks at his fleas; a dog hunting does not notice them'

'Men in the game are blind to what men looking on see clearly'

'The first time it is a favour, the second time a rule'

RUSSIAN

'An old loan repaid is like finding something new'

'Don't worry if you borrow, but worry if you lend'

'They bow to you when borrowing, you bow to them when collecting'

'Many who have gold in the house are looking for copper outside'

'Golden hands, but a wicked mouth'

'The coat is quite new, only the holes are old'

'A lizard on a cushion will still seek leaves'

'They gave the naked man a shirt and he said it was too thick'

'It is easy to undress the naked'

'After the head is off, one does not cry over the hair'

'Small children give you headache; big children heartache'

'With seven nurses the child loses its eye'

'As long as a child does not cry, it does not matter what pleases it'

'He that is afraid of bad luck will never know good'

'Bad luck is fertile'

'When roubles fall from heaven there is no sack, when there is a sack roubles don't fall'

'There is plenty of sound in an empty barrel'

'A jug that has been mended lasts two hundred years'

'In the kingdom of hope there is no winter'

'The horses of hope gallop, but the asses of experience go slowly'

'One son is no son, two sons is no son, but three sons is a son'

'An indispensable thing never has much value'

'A field held in common is always ravaged by bears'

'The wife is twice precious only; when led into the house, and when taken out'

'To run away is not glorious, but very healthy'

'He that hath no heart, let him have heels'

'It is good to sleep in a whole skin'

'If you put your nose into water, you will also wet your cheeks'

'No one is dragged to heaven by the hair'

'Happiness is not a horse, you cannot harness it'

SPANISH

'In the street of by-and-by one arrives at the house of "never"'

'God comes to see without ringing the bell'

'Punishment is a cripple, but it arrives'

'Between two Saturday's happen many marvels'

'Beads about the neck, and the devil in the heart'

'I dance to the tune that is played'

'It is better to weep with wise men than to laugh with fools'

'Every cask smells of the wine it contained'

'He who knows nothing, doubts nothing'

'The fear of women is the basis of good health'

'The only chaste woman is the one who has not been chased'

'An ounce of blood is worth more than a pound of friendship'

'Between brothers, two witnesses and a notary'

'It is good to have friends, even in hell'

'A good man's pedigree is little hunted up'

'A friend to everybody and to nobody is the same thing'

'The best mirror is an old friend'

'The world is a round gulf, and he who cannot swim must go to the bottom'

'Who ties well, unties well'

'God gives almonds to those who have no teeth'

'Halfway is twelve miles when you have fourteen miles to go'

'A good grievance is better than bad payment'

'If the sky falls, hold up your hands'

'Better a quiet death than a public misfortune'

'Even a sick man shuns death'

INDIAN

'One "no" averts seventy evils'

'The sieve says to the needle; you have a hole in your head'

'When you are in the water you swim'

'Don't judge any man until you have walked two moons in his moccasins'

And a very prosaic proverb which sums up a complete code of behaviour . . .

'Charity done in secret, eager courtesy to the visitor of his house, silence after doing kindness and public mention after receiving it. Modesty in fortune, conversation without the spice of insolence. Who taught good men this rule of life, hard as a sword's edge to tread?'

'Be first at the feast, and last at the fight'

'A guilty conscience is a hidden enemy'

'Do not blame God for having created the tiger, but thank him for not having given it wings'

ARABIAN

'Better a handful of dry dates and content therewith than to own the Gate of Peacocks and be kicked in the eye by a broody camel'

'Think of the going out before you enter'

'Nothing but a handful of dust will fill the eyes of man'

'Better a hundred enemies outside the house than one inside'

'All strangers are relations to each other'

'Live together like brothers and do business like strangers'

'A wise man associating with the vicious becomes an idiot; a dog travelling with good men becomes a rational being'

'The dogs bark, but the caravan moves on'

'If the camel once gets his nose in the tent, his body will follow'

'A thousand curses never tore a shirt'

'One is better off seated than standing, lying than seated, asleep than awake, and dead than alive'

'There are no fans in hell'

'Let the sword decide after stratagem has failed'

'The sinning is the best part of repentance'

'The barber learns his trade on the orphan's chin'

'If I were to trade in winding sheets, no one would die'

'If you buy cheap meat, when it boils you smell what you have saved'

MALAY

'Kick away the ladder and one's feet are left dangling'

'The body pays for a slip of the foot, and gold pays for a slip of the tongue'

'Fear to let fall a drop and you will spill a lot'

'It is the fate of the coconut husk to float, for the stone to sink'

'A lost wife can be replaced, but the loss of character spells ruin'

'He that can see a louse as far away as China is unconscious of an elephant on his nose'

'Trumpet in a herd of elephants,
Crow in the company of cocks,
Bleat in a flock of goats'

'A diplomat should be yielding and supple as a liana that can be bent but not broken'

'As a bamboo conduit makes a round jet of water, so taking counsel together rounds men to one mind'

'To depend on one's own child is blindness in one eye;
To depend on a stranger, blindness in both eyes'

'The cradle is rocked but the baby is pinched'

'When the curry is good, the rice is half cooked;
When the rice is good, the curry is half cooked . . .'

ITALIAN

'Teeth placed before the tongue give good advice'

'Half a brain is enough for him who says little'

'Have an open face but conceal your thoughts'

'In buying a horse and taking a wife, shut your eyes and
commend yourself to God'

'For a wife and a horse go to your neighbour'

'Praise a maid in the morning, and the weather at night'

'She who is born a beauty is born betrothed'

'Trifles make perfection, but perfection is no trifle'

'Tell not all you know, believe not all you hear, do not all
you are able'

'One may have good eyes and yet see nothing'

'There is no need to bind up one's head before it is broken'

'A favour to come is better than a hundred received'

'Who offends writes on sand; who is offended, on marble'

'To a covered ill an open razor'

'Trouble rides a fast horse'

'He would share even his share of the sun'

'He who begins many things finishes but few'

'When the sun is highest it casts the least shadow'

'What does not poison fattens'

'Who sows thorns should not go barefoot'

'At a dangerous passage, yield to precedence'

'Land was never lost for want of an heir'

'A runaway monk never praises his monastery'

'He who wants a great deal must not ask for a little'

GREEK

Many proverbs actually have Greek origin, some are very old:

'Men prone to tears are good'

'To the brave man every land is a native country'

'Seize the end and you will hold the middle'

'Add not fire to fire'

'Thinking evil is much the same as doing it'

'A small evil may be a great good'

'Act quickly, think slowly'

'A miser is ever in want'

'Nothing will content him who is not content with a little'

'Hunger is the teacher of many'

'Don't hear one and judge two'

'A word out of season may mar a whole lifetime'

'Neither promise wax to the saint, nor cakes to the child'

'He who laughs not in the morning, laughs not at noon'

'Poor men's words have little weight'

'There's many a slip 'twixt the cup and the lip'

'It is the men who make a city'

'In hospitality it is the spirit that counts'

'Welcome is the best cheer'

'Those who are thirsty drink in silence'

'The shepherd, even when he becomes a gentleman, smells of lamb'

'With a relation eat and drink; but conduct no business with him'

'The silence of a treacherous man is to be feared even more than his words'

'Wood that grows warped can never be straightened'

'Affairs sleep soundly when fortune is present'

'Endeavour to bear the ignorance of fortune with patience'

'The mills of the gods grind slowly, but they grind exceeding small'

TURKISH

These may be nearly as old as the Greek proverbs . . .

'The hand that gives is above the hand that takes'

'Remember, two watermelons cannot be held under one arm'

'Satan's friendship reaches to the prison door'

'Be thine enemy an ant, see in him an elephant'

'Anyone can kill a trussed foe'

'Accept the largesse of thy friend as though he were an enemy'

'He became an infidel hesitating between two mosques'

'A weapon is an enemy even to its owner'

'The devil tempts all other men, but idle men tempt the devil'

'Fall not into the fire to avoid smoke'

'Smoke does not make a pot boil'

'A camel's kick, soft but stunning'

'A sheik's miracles are of his own telling'

'Measure a thousand times and cut once'

'Insolent ones are never without wounds'

'The courteous one learns his courtesy from the discourteous'

'No camel route is long, with good company'

'No rose without a thorn, or a love without a rival'

'He that conceals his grief finds no remedy for it'

'Coffee should be black as hell; strong as death, and sweet as love'

JAPANESE

The Japanese proverbs that follow are much shorter than those of the Chinese, but nonetheless meaningful . . .

'Ten men, ten minds'

'Proof rather than argument'

'Breeding rather than birth'

'The tongue is more to be feared than the sword'

'Life is for one generation; a good name is forever'

'If you wait, there will come nectar — like fair weather'

'A single arrow is easily broken, but not ten in a bundle'

'A statement once let loose cannot be caught by four horses'

'Wisdom and virtue are like the two wheels of a cart'

'To kick with sore toe only hurts foot'

'To endure what is unendurable is true endurance'

'Wine is the best broom for troubles'

'Don't rejoice over him that goes, before you see him that comes'

'When folly passes by, reason draws back'

'The acolyte at the gate reads scriptures he has never learnt'

'Not to know is to be a Buddha'

Two rather cynical ones...

> 'Never trust a woman, even if she has borne you seven children'

> 'If I peddle salt, it rains; if I peddle flour, the wind blows'

——————— NORTH AMERICAN ———————

Benjamin Franklin (1706-90) the well-known American states-man and philosopher, was very partial to proverbs, many he invented himself, others he collected and included them in his famous almanack; here are some of them. Naturally, as may be said of many famous people, it is not really possible to know positively which proverbial sayings they were actually responsible for. However, here are some proverbs taken from his famous almanack — well known to us as 'Poor Richard's Almanack'...

> 'He that lives on hope will die fasting'

> 'Be in general virtuous, and you will be happy'

> 'Reading makes a full man, meditation a profound man, discourse a clear man'

> 'Without justice, courage is weak'

> 'If you desire many things, many things will beseem but a few'

> 'A benevolent man should allow a few faults in himself to keep his friends in countenance'

> 'To be proud of knowledge is to be blind with light'

> 'Laws too gentle are seldom obeyed; too severe, seldom executed'

> 'Keep your eyes wide open before marriage, half shut afterwards'

> 'You can bear with your own faults, and why not a fault in your wife?'

> 'Necessity never made a good bargain'

> 'Would you persuade, speak of interest, not of reason'

> 'Pride is said to be the last vice the good man gets clear of'

'Pride that dines on vanity sups on contempt'

'If you ride a horse, sit close and tight,
If you ride a man, sit easy and light'

Other American proverbs . . .

'Folks like the truth that hits their neighbour'

'There's no fun in physic, but a good deal of physic in fun'

'You cannot unscramble eggs'

'Feel for others, in your pocket'

'Where the woman wears the breeches, she has a good right to them'

'Wishes won't wash dishes'

'Opportunities, like eggs, come one at a time'

'Hope is a good breakfast, but a poor supper'

—————————— PORTUGUESE ——————————

The following are not unlike those of China, rather subtle, but nevertheless full of good advice . . .

'Money lent, is an enemy made'

'Where the iron goes, there goes also rust'

'Peace with a cudgel in hand is war'

'Where there is no might right loses itself'

'Better a red face than a black heart'

'Visits always give pleasure; if not the arriving, so the departing'

'What is bought is cheaper than a gift'

'Prosperity lets the bridle go'

'Never cut what can be untied'

'There's no catching trouts with dry breeches'

'If you have no enemies, then fortune passed you by'

'Don't tie a knot in your tongue that you cannot untie with your teeth'

'He that would speak the truth must have one foot in the stirrup'

IRISH

And, lastly, a few proverbs that are not lacking in humour . . .

'A new broom sweeps clean, but the old brush knows all the corners'

'It is not easy to steal where the landlord is a thief'

'The man that sits on the bank always hurls well'

'A house can't be kept without talk'

'There is pain in prohibition'

'Anything will fit a naked man'

'Every invalid is a physician'

'Keep a thing for seven years and you'll find a use for it'

'Comfort is not known if poverty does not come before it'

'Evening is speedier than morning'

'A good denial, the best point in law'

'A service not asked for, neither God nor man is thankful for'

'Your own deeds will long be baptized on you'

'Sweet is the wine but sour is the payment'

'Where the tongue slips, it speaks the truth'

'Nearest the heart comes first out'

'One must pay Health its tithes'

'It is not fish until it is on the bank'

'One leg in the stocks, or two, 'tis all the same'

'If you loan your breeches don't cut off the buttons'

'A bald head is soon shaven'

'What's got badly, goes badly'

'He who is bad at giving lodgings is good at showing the way'

'It's almost as good as bringing good news not to bring bad'

'Your neighbour will never make a good boundary fence'

INDEX

Actors, 48
Advice, 10-11
Aesop's Fables, 9
Age, 118-120
All Hallows, 126
Ambitions, 13
Amerindian sayings, 97
Amiel, Henri Frederic, 109
Anger, 8
Ants, 105-106
Arabia, 137-138
Artists, 49
Asses, 92
Autumn, 126

Bacon, Francis, 8, 34, 72, 113, 117
Bast, 93
Bears, 103
Bees, 105-106
Beggars, 36-37
Berkshire, 98
Bible, the, 8, 9, 11, 12, 34, 46, 58, 67, 80, 102, 119, 123, 129, 131
Bierce, Ambrose, 8, 13, 80
Birds, 86
Blake, William, 8, 188, 96, 102
Borrowing, 17-18
Browning, Robert, 48, 91
Bryant, William, 77
Burns, Robert, 59
Butler, Samuel, 42, 83, 121

Canada, 84
Candlemas, 64
Carlyle, Thomas, 55
Carroll, Lewis, 45
Cats, 92-94
Childhood, 109-110
China, 82, 92, 132-133
Christmas, 127-128
Coleridge, Samuel Taylor, 130
Colton, Charles Caleb, 10, 101
Confucius, 12, 32, 45, 113, 132-133
Congreve, William, 130
Country sayings, 64-65, 75-76
Cowley, Abraham, 114
Cows, 94
Crows, 87
Cuckoo, 87-88

Dante, 63
Death, 120-121
Devil, the, 72, 82-85
Devon, 91
Dickens, Charles, 41, 44, 56
Dickinson, Emily, 8, 87, 107, 121
Disraeli, Benjamin, 116
Doctors, 39-41
Dogs, 94-96
Donne, John, 107
Druids, 71
Dryden, John, 131

Eagles, 88
Egypt, 93, 104
Eliot, George, 92
Emerson, Ralph Waldo,
    19, 25, 63, 120, 131
Euripides, 119
Evil, 80-81
Evil Eye, 81-82
Exodus, 79
Experience, 18, 19

Fielding, Henry, 40
Fishermen, 27
Fishing, 28-29
Fleas, 106-107
Flies, 106-107
Flowers, 58-59
Fog, 72-73
Fools, 51-52
Fortune, 15-16
Fox, 96-97
France, Anatole, 122
Franklin, Benjamin, 7, 42, 44,
    144
Friendship, 14-15
Fuller, Thomas, 16, 20, 23,
    33, 34, 36, 40, 43, 45, 50,
    56, 101, 107, 120, 123, 129

Garden lore, 58-59
Geese, 88
Gipsies, 87, 98-99
Goldsmith, Oliver, 119
Gracian, Baltasar, 113
Grass, 62
Graves, Robert, 121
Greece, 140-141
Guiterman, Arthur, 106
Gulls, 29-30

Hampshire, 70, 88
Hardy, Thomas, 113
Hares, 103
Harlots, 53
Harvest, 125-126
Hawthorne, Nathaniel,
    59, 122
Health, 22
Hebrew sayings, 17, 71, 81
Hens, 89
Herbert, George, 92
Herbs, 61-62
Hermant, Abel, 20
Herrick, Robert, 60
Heywood, John, 37
Hill, Aaron, 61
Holmes, Oliver Wendell, 44,
    46, 48
Honesty, 19-20
Horses, 97-100
Howe, Edgar Watson, 11,
    17, 52
Hugo, Victor, 16

India, 97, 137
Ireland, 146-147
Italy, 139

Japan, 143-144, 82
Jerome, Jerome K., 115
Jesters, 51
Jesus, 62, 91
Johnson, Samuel, 9, 32, 114
Jonahs, 31
Jonson, Ben, 43

Kings, 47-48
Knowledge, 12

Lambs, 100
Lateness, 7

Lawyers, 41-43
Learning, 12-13
Lending, 17-18
Leonardo Da Vinci, 15
Leopards, 101
Lions, 101
Longfellow, Henry, 8, 13, 21, 52, 120, 129
Love, 113-115

Magpies, 89
Malay, 138-139
Marcello, Benedetto, 48
Marlowe, Christopher, 48
Marriage, 115-117
Maughan, William Somerset, 119
Mice, 101
Milton, John, 46, 63
Mists, 72
Molière, 40, 50, 52
Moon, 70-71
More, Sir Thomas, 61
Mothers-in-law, 117-118
Musicians, 52

Napoleon, 47
Nature, 62-63
Nelson, Horatio, 30
Nettles, 60-61
New Forest, 118
Nietzsche, 37
Norsemen, 67-68
North America, 144-145

Old English sayings, 110
Omar Khayyam, 112
Ovid, 60
Owls, 90
Oxen, 104

Parents, 110-111
Peacocks, 90
Penn, William, 46
Pigeons, 90
Pigs, 102-103
Poets, 44-45
Politicians, 44
Poor man, 34-36
Pope, Alexander, 123
Portugal, 145-146
Priests, 43-44
Prince Regent, 25

Rabbits, 103
Rain, 65-70
Rainbow, 67-68
Rats, 104-105
Ravens, 91
Riddles, 28, 29, 55, 68, 71, 72, 97, 125, 128
Rich man, 32-34
Robins, 91
Rochefoucauld, Francois, 112, 119
Roses, 59-60
Ross, James, 94
Russell, Bertrand, 106
Russia, 133-134

Sailors, 24-26
St Swithin, 56, 66
Scotland, 38, 89
Sea lore, 24-26
Sea-sickness, 28
Seasons, 123
Secrets, 17
Servants, 46-47
Shakespeare, William, 8, 27, 35, 38, 41, 47, 53, 63, 67, 68, 82, 88, 129

Sheep, 9
Shelley, Percy Bysshe, 47, 77
Shepherds, 100
Ships, 24-26
Silence, 20-21
Sleep, 22-23
Smith, Sydney, 43
Sophocles, 44, 110
Spain, 135-136
Spiders, 107
Spring, 123
Stevenson, Robert Louis, 53, 110, 123
Storms, 69-70
Summer, 124
Sun, 71-72
Swallows, 9
Sympathy, 16-17

Tailors, 49-50
Talmud, The, 14, 20
Teachers, 45-46
Tennyson, Alfred Lord, 12, 18, 123, 128
Thief, 37-39
Thistles, 61
Thunder, 69
Tides, 27

Tigers, 8
Time, 122
Trees, 54-58
Truth, 9-10
Turkey, 142-143
Twain, Mark, 8, 14, 21, 51, 53, 84

Voltaire, 105

Walton, Izaac, 22
Ward, Henry Beecher, 36, 42, 50, 110
Watts, Isaac, 51, 95
Weather, 64-65, 73
Weeds, 60
Widows, 117
Wilde, Oscar, 13, 119
Wind, 68
Winter, 127, 77
Wisdom, 11-12
Witches 79-80
Wolf, 105
Writers, 53

Yesterday, 131
Youth, 111-113